9th Grade Wo

lables.com
.om
- thesaurus.com

Use the dictionary to write the definition and divide the words for each day below into syllables.

Amphibian: **Week 1**

○ MONDAY **WORD:** *Dwarf Siren*

EXAMPLE:

Dwarf sirens are eel-like salamanders.

dwarf si-ren

TUESDAY **WORD: Crested Newt**

WEDNESDAY **WORD: Disc-Tongued Frog**

THURSDAY **WORD: Amphiuma**

FRIDAY **WORD: Caecilian**

SATURDAY / SUNDAY **WORD: Brook Salamander**

Write Words In ABC Order

Dwarf Siren

For each word, find one synonym & one antonym. (if none: write word + none)

Dwarf Siren - none

9th Grade Word of The Day

Use the dictionary to write the definition and divide the words for each day below into syllables.

WEEK 2

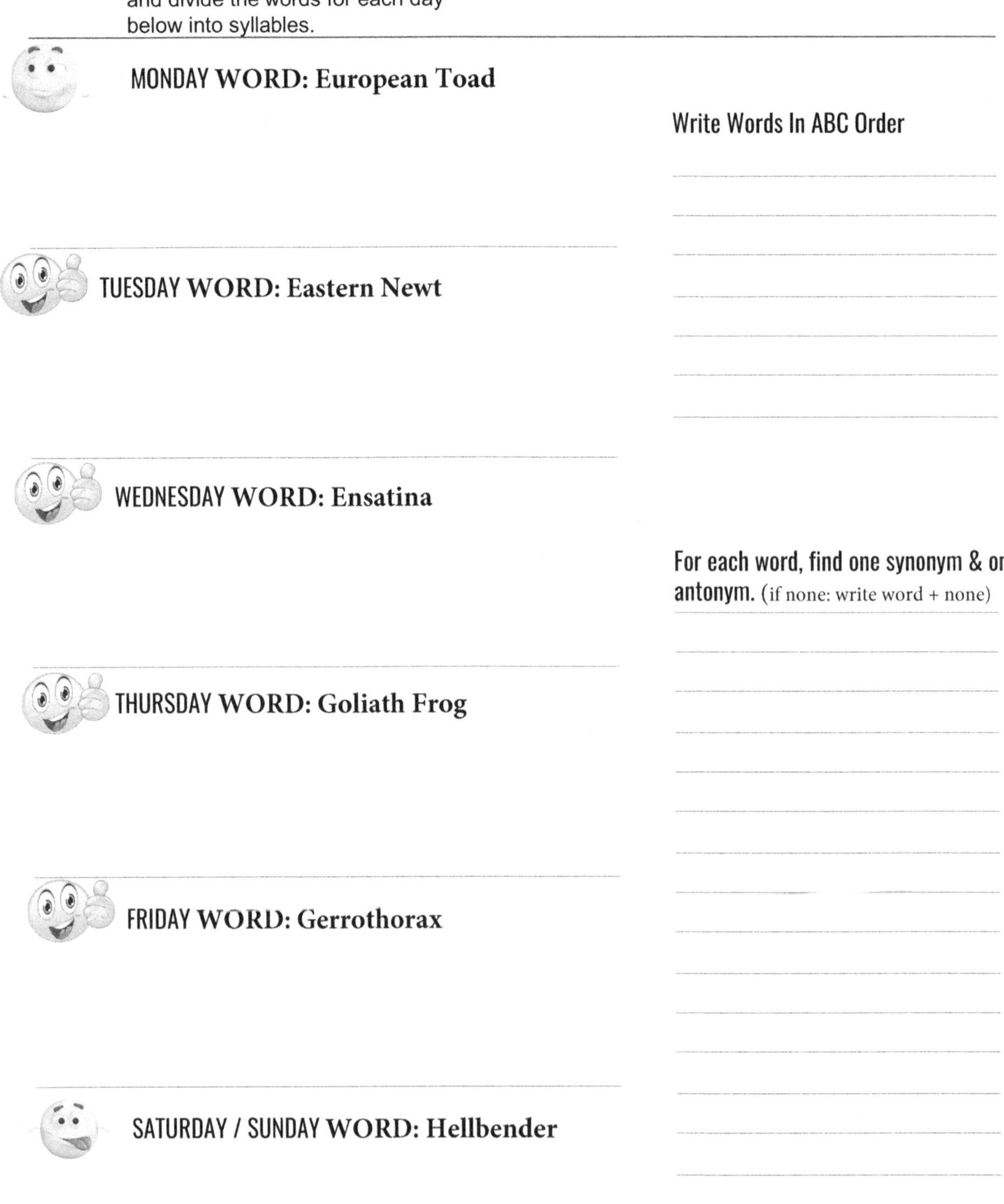

MONDAY **WORD: European Toad**

TUESDAY **WORD: Eastern Newt**

WEDNESDAY **WORD: Ensatina**

THURSDAY **WORD: Goliath Frog**

FRIDAY **WORD: Gerrothorax**

SATURDAY / SUNDAY **WORD: Hellbender**

Write Words In ABC Order

For each word, find one synonym & one antonym. (if none: write word + none)

9th Grade Word of The Day

Use the dictionary to write the definition and divide the words for each day below into syllables.

WEEK 3

MONDAY **WORD: Knobby Newt**

TUESDAY **WORD: Mantella Frog**

WEDNESDAY **WORD: Knot Of Toads**

THURSDAY **WORD: Clipper Ship**

FRIDAY **WORD: Moss Frog**

SATURDAY / SUNDAY **WORD:**
Mudpuppy
Mexican Treefrog

Write Words In ABC Order

For each word, find one synonym & one antonym. (if none: write word + none)

9th Grade Word of The Day

Use the dictionary to write the definition and divide the words for each day below into syllables.

WEEK 4

MONDAY **WORD: Polliwog**

TUESDAY **WORD: Spadefoot**

WEDNESDAY **WORD: Western Toad**

THURSDAY **WORD: Tongueless Frog**

FRIDAY **WORD: Waterdog**

SATURDAY / SUNDAY **WORD: Tetrapod Vertebrates**

Write Words In ABC Order

For each word, find one synonym & one antonym. (if none: write word + none)

9th Grade Word of The Day

Use the dictionary to write the definition and divide the words for each day below into syllables.

Transportation: **WEEK 5**

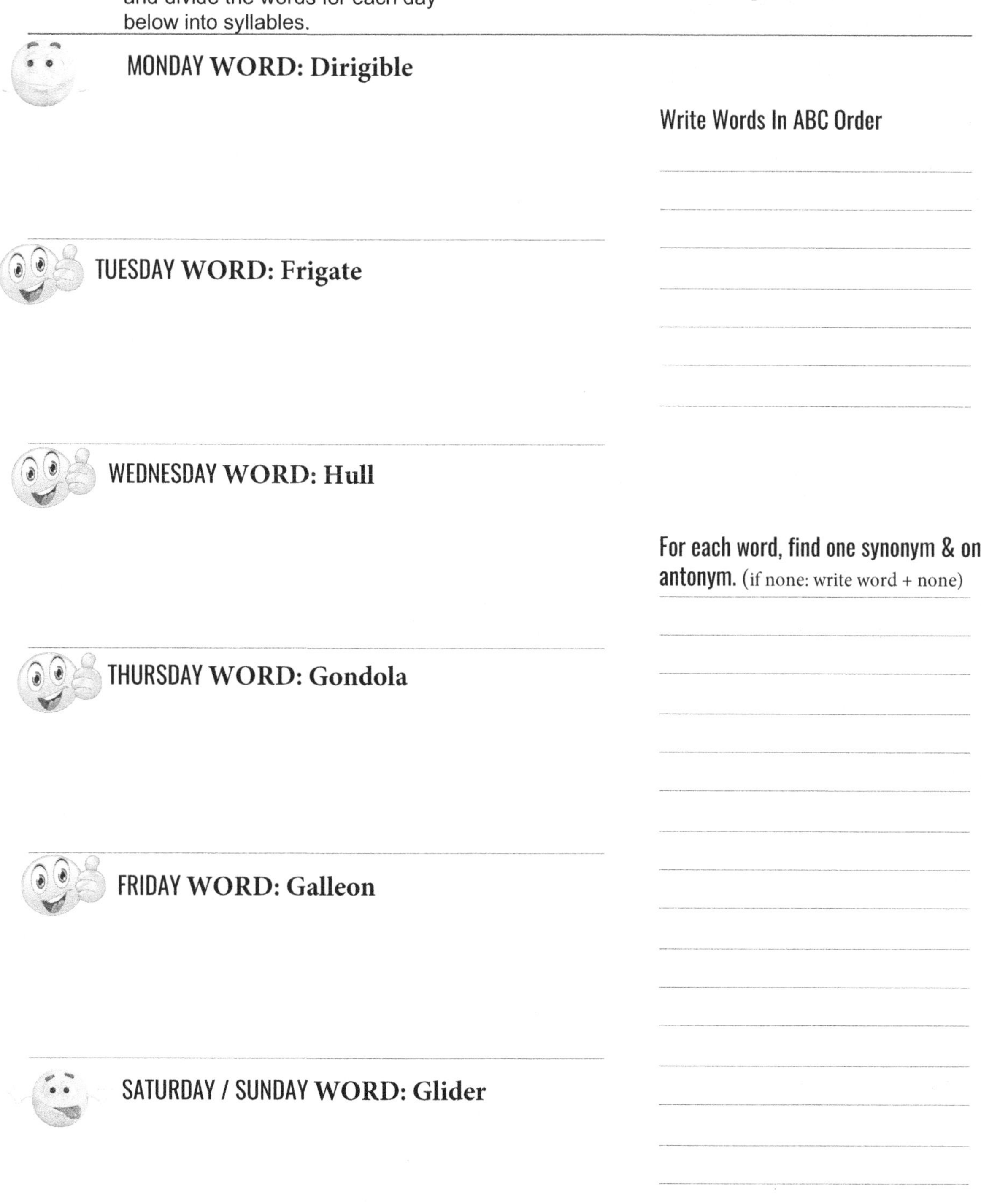

MONDAY **WORD: Dirigible**

TUESDAY **WORD: Frigate**

WEDNESDAY **WORD: Hull**

THURSDAY **WORD: Gondola**

FRIDAY **WORD: Galleon**

SATURDAY / SUNDAY **WORD: Glider**

Write Words In ABC Order

For each word, find one synonym & one antonym. (if none: write word + none)

9th Grade Word of The Day

Use the dictionary to write the definition and divide the words for each day below into syllables.

WEEK 6

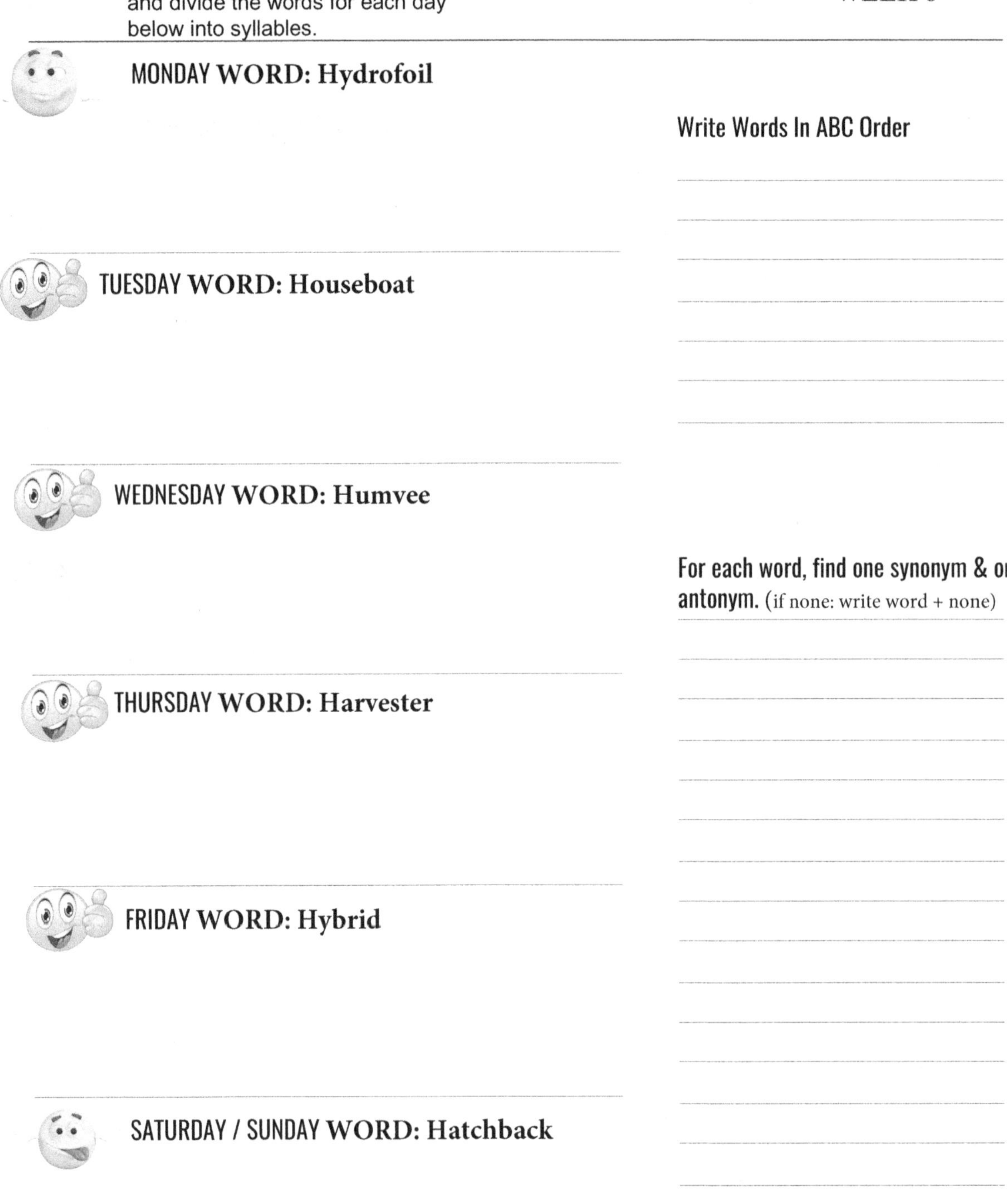

MONDAY **WORD: Hydrofoil**

TUESDAY **WORD: Houseboat**

WEDNESDAY **WORD: Humvee**

THURSDAY **WORD: Harvester**

FRIDAY **WORD: Hybrid**

SATURDAY / SUNDAY **WORD: Hatchback**

Write Words In ABC Order

For each word, find one synonym & one antonym. (if none: write word + none)

9th Grade Word of The Day

Use the dictionary to write the definition and divide the words for each day below into syllables.

WEEK 7

MONDAY **WORD: Hydroplane**

TUESDAY **WORD: Hearse**

WEDNESDAY **WORD: Hansom Cab**

THURSDAY **WORD: Jalopy**

FRIDAY **WORD: Hovercraft**

SATURDAY / SUNDAY **WORD: Jetliner**

Write Words In ABC Order

For each word, find one synonym & one antonym. (if none: write word + none)

9th Grade Word of The Day

Use the dictionary to write the definition and divide the words for each day below into syllables.

WEEK 8

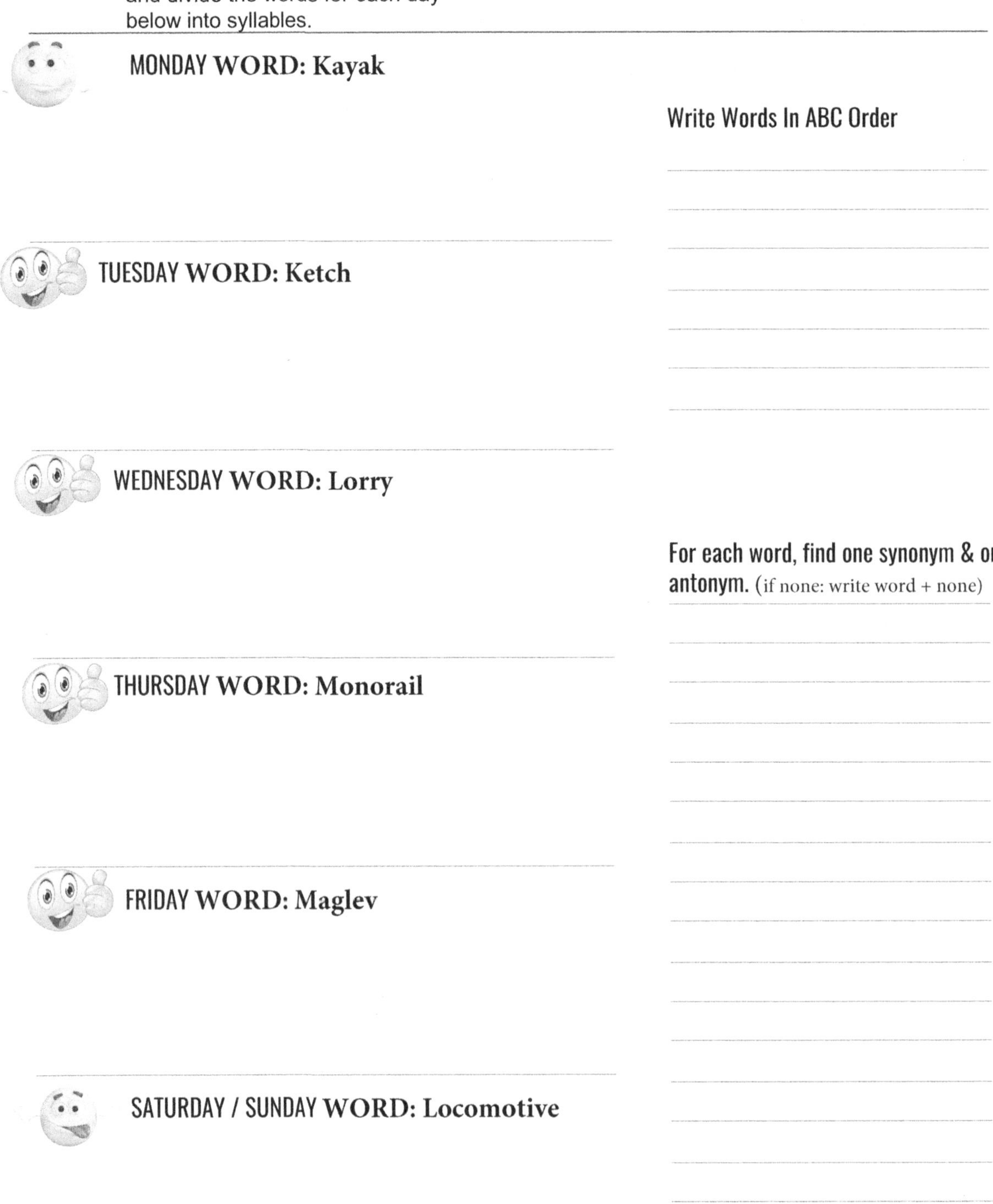

MONDAY WORD: Kayak
TUESDAY WORD: Ketch
WEDNESDAY WORD: Lorry
THURSDAY WORD: Monorail
FRIDAY WORD: Maglev
SATURDAY / SUNDAY WORD: Locomotive
Write Words In ABC Order
For each word, find one synonym & one antonym. (if none: write word + none)

9th Grade Word of The Day

Use the dictionary to write the definition and divide the words for each day below into syllables.

WEEK 9

MONDAY **WORD: Minesweeper**

TUESDAY **WORD: Narrowboat**

WEDNESDAY **WORD: Propeller**

THURSDAY **WORD: Outrigger Canoe**

FRIDAY **WORD: Prairie Schooner**

SATURDAY / SUNDAY **WORD: Oxcart & Ragtop**

Write Words In ABC Order

For each word, find one synonym & one antonym. (if none: write word + none)

9th Grade Word of The Day

Use the dictionary to write the definition and divide the words for each day below into syllables.

WEEK 10

MONDAY WORD: **Rapid Transit**

TUESDAY WORD: **Roadster**

WEDNESDAY WORD: **Rickshaw**

THURSDAY WORD: **Rudder**

FRIDAY WORD: **Surrey**

SATURDAY / SUNDAY WORD: **Ski Lift**

Write Words In ABC Order

For each word, find one synonym & one antonym. (if none: write word + none)

9th Grade Word of The Day

Use the dictionary to write the definition and divide the words for each day below into syllables.

WEEK 11

MONDAY **WORD: Seaplane**

TUESDAY **WORD: Stagecoach**

WEDNESDAY **WORD: Sledge**

THURSDAY **WORD: Segway**

FRIDAY **WORD: Steamship**

SATURDAY / SUNDAY **WORD: Skiff**

Write Words In ABC Order

For each word, find one synonym & one antonym. (if none: write word + none)

9th Grade Word of The Day

Use the dictionary to write the definition and divide the words for each day below into syllables.

WEEK 12

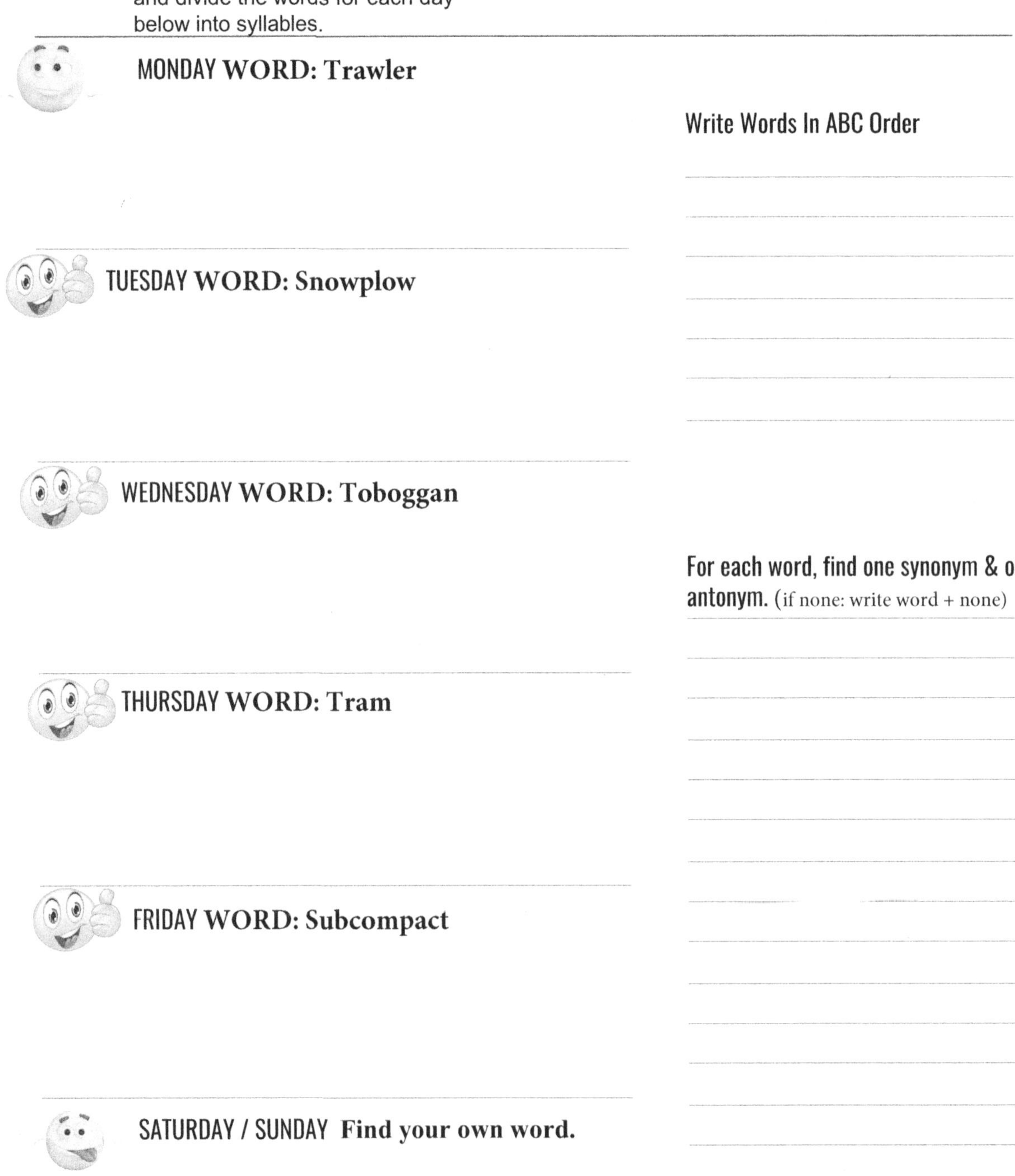

MONDAY WORD: Trawler
Write Words In ABC Order
TUESDAY WORD: Snowplow
WEDNESDAY WORD: Toboggan
For each word, find one synonym & one antonym. (if none: write word + none)
THURSDAY WORD: Tram
FRIDAY WORD: Subcompact
SATURDAY / SUNDAY Find your own word.

9th Grade Word of The Day

Use the dictionary to write the definition and divide the words for each day below into syllables.

WEEK 13

MONDAY **WORD: Vespa**

Write Words In ABC Order

TUESDAY **WORD: Windjammer**

WEDNESDAY **WORD: Thresher**

For each word, find one synonym & one antonym. (if none: write word + none)

THURSDAY **WORD: Zamboni**

FRIDAY **WORD: Yawl**

SATURDAY / SUNDAY **WORD: Tugboat**

9th Grade Word of The Day

Use the dictionary to write the definition and divide the words for each day below into syllables.

Colors: WEEK 14

MONDAY **WORD: Amethyst**

TUESDAY **WORD: Apricot**

WEDNESDAY **WORD: Aquamarine**

THURSDAY **WORD: Gamboge**

FRIDAY **WORD: Fandango**

SATURDAY / SUNDAY **WORD: Crimson**

Write Words In ABC Order

For each word, find one synonym & one antonym. (if none: write word + none)

9th Grade Word of The Day

Use the dictionary to write the definition and divide the words for each day below into syllables.

WEEK 15

MONDAY **WORD: Coquelicot**

TUESDAY **WORD: Smaragdine**

WEDNESDAY **WORD: Fuchsia**

THURSDAY **WORD: Magenta**

FRIDAY **WORD: Feldgrau**

SATURDAY / SUNDAY **WORD: Wenge**

Write Words In ABC Order

For each word, find one synonym & one antonym. (if none: write word + none)

9th Grade Word of The Day

Use the dictionary to write the definition and divide the words for each day below into syllables.

WEEK 16

MONDAY **WORD: Cyan**

TUESDAY **WORD: Cordovan**

WEDNESDAY **WORD: Fulvous**

THURSDAY **WORD: Brazilwood**

FRIDAY **WORD: Cadmium Yellow**

SATURDAY / SUNDAY **WORD:**
Australien & Bastard Amber

Write Words In ABC Order

For each word, find one synonym & one antonym. (if none: write word + none)

9th Grade Word of The Day

Use the dictionary to write the definition and divide the words for each day below into syllables.

Science: WEEK 17

MONDAY **WORD: Astrophysics**

TUESDAY **WORD: Botany**

WEDNESDAY **WORD: Climatologist**

THURSDAY **WORD: Cuvette**

FRIDAY **WORD: Datum**

SATURDAY / SUNDAY **WORD: Electrochemist**

Write Words In ABC Order

For each word, find one synonym & one antonym. (if none: write word + none)

9th Grade Word of The Day

Use the dictionary to write the definition and divide the words for each day below into syllables.

WEEK 18

9th Grade Word of The Day

Use the dictionary to write the definition and divide the words for each day below into syllables.

WEEK 19

MONDAY **WORD: Mineralogy**

TUESDAY **WORD: Paleontology**

WEDNESDAY **WORD: Ornithology**

THURSDAY **WORD: Petri Dish**

FRIDAY **WORD: Photosynthesis**

SATURDAY / SUNDAY **WORD: Pipette**

Write Words In ABC Order

For each word, find one synonym & one antonym. (if none: write word + none)

9th Grade Word of The Day

Use the dictionary to write the definition and divide the words for each day below into syllables.

WEEK 20

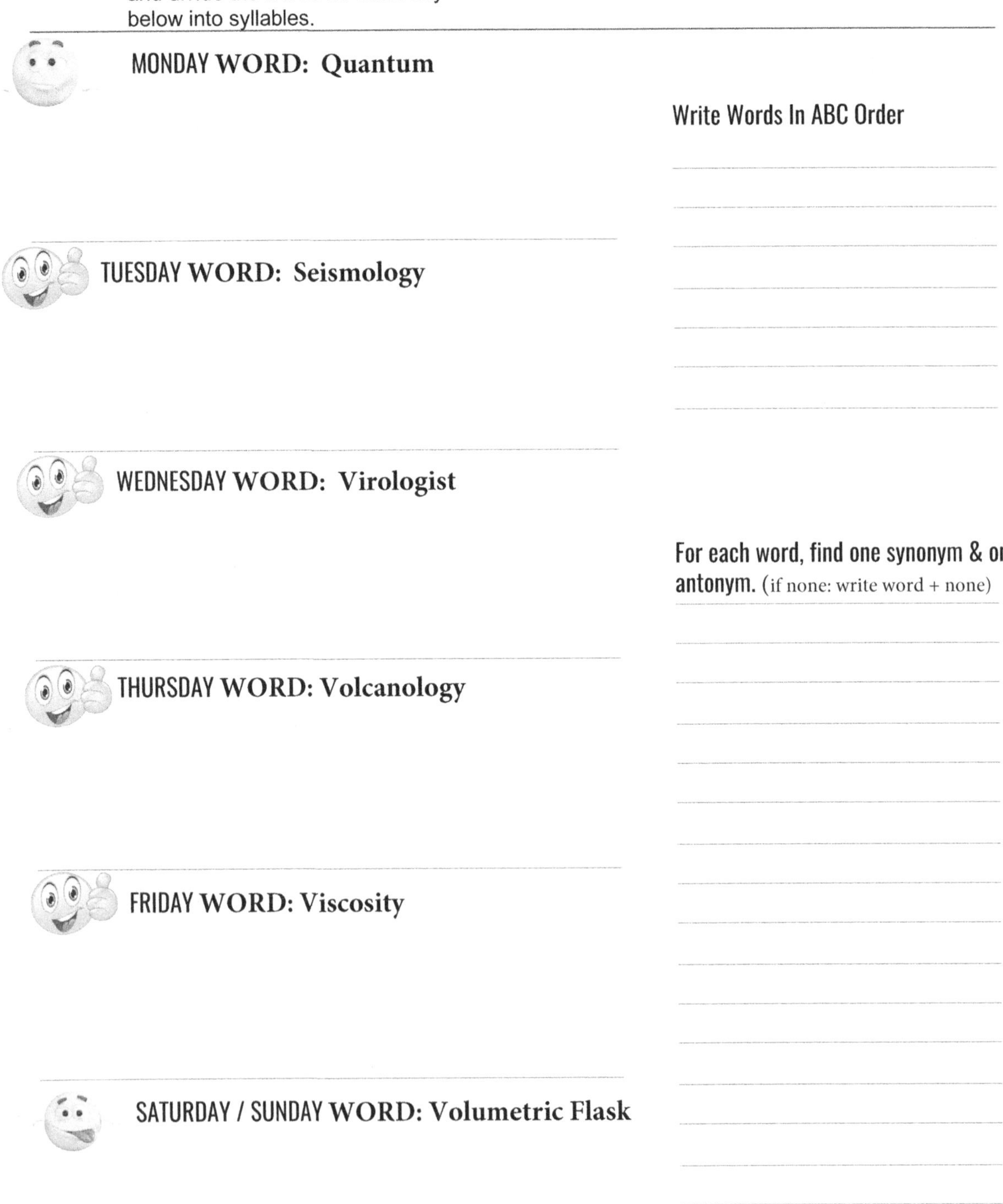

MONDAY WORD: Quantum
TUESDAY WORD: Seismology
WEDNESDAY WORD: Virologist
THURSDAY WORD: Volcanology
FRIDAY WORD: Viscosity
SATURDAY / SUNDAY WORD: Volumetric Flask
Write Words In ABC Order
For each word, find one synonym & one antonym. (if none: write word + none)

9th Grade Word of The Day

Use the dictionary to write the definition and divide the words for each day below into syllables.

Random: WEEK 21

MONDAY **WORD: Lullaby**

TUESDAY **WORD: Sovereign**

WEDNESDAY **WORD: Propagandize**

THURSDAY **WORD: Gourmand**

FRIDAY **WORD: Zealous**

SATURDAY / SUNDAY **WORD: Filibuster**

Write Words In ABC Order

For each word, find one synonym & one antonym. (if none: write word + none)

9th Grade Word of The Day

Use the dictionary to write the definition and divide the words for each day below into syllables.

WEEK 22

MONDAY **WORD: Chauvinism**

Write Words In ABC Order

TUESDAY **WORD: Carburetor**

WEDNESDAY **WORD: Accordion**

For each word, find one synonym & one antonym. (if none: write word + none)

THURSDAY **WORD: Chocolaty**

FRIDAY **WORD: Coolly**

SATURDAY / SUNDAY **WORD: Defiant**

9th Grade Word of The Day

Use the dictionary to write the definition and divide the words for each day below into syllables.

WEEK 23

MONDAY **WORD: Deterrence**

TUESDAY **WORD: Desiccate**

WEDNESDAY **WORD: Diorama**

THURSDAY **WORD: Dissipate**

FRIDAY **WORD: Flotation**

SATURDAY / SUNDAY **WORD: Guttural**

Write Words In ABC Order

For each word, find one synonym & one antonym. (if none: write word + none)

9th Grade Word of The Day

Use the dictionary to write the definition and divide the words for each day below into syllables.

WEEK 24

MONDAY **WORD: Hypocrisy**

TUESDAY **WORD: Inadvertent**

WEDNESDAY **WORD: Irascible**

THURSDAY **WORD: Ingenious**

FRIDAY **WORD: Lieutenant**

SATURDAY / SUNDAY **WORD: Liquefy**

Write Words In ABC Order

For each word, find one synonym & one antonym. (if none: write word + none)

9th Grade Word of The Day

Use the dictionary to write the definition and divide the words for each day below into syllables.

WEEK 25

MONDAY **WORD: Mischief**

TUESDAY **WORD: Onomatopoeia**

WEDNESDAY **WORD: Misogyny**

THURSDAY **WORD: Plenitude**

FRIDAY **WORD: Presumptuous**

SATURDAY / SUNDAY **WORD: Parliament**

Write Words In ABC Order

For each word, find one synonym & one antonym. (if none: write word + none)

9th Grade Word of The Day

Use the dictionary to write the definition and divide the words for each day below into syllables.

WEEK 26

MONDAY **WORD: Puerile**

Write Words In ABC Order

TUESDAY **WORD: Propagate**

WEDNESDAY **WORD: Sacrilegious**

For each word, find one synonym & one antonym. (if none: write word + none)

THURSDAY **WORD: Putrefy**

FRIDAY **WORD: Septuagenarian**

SATURDAY / SUNDAY **WORD: Shish Kebab**

9th Grade Word of The Day

Use the dictionary to write the definition and divide the words for each day below into syllables.

Jobs: WEEK 27

MONDAY **WORD: Ambassador**

TUESDAY **WORD: Auctioneer**

WEDNESDAY **WORD: Cartographer**

THURSDAY **WORD: Cardiologist**

FRIDAY **WORD: Clergywoman**

SATURDAY / SUNDAY **WORD: Calligrapher**

Write Words In ABC Order

For each word, find one synonym & one antonym. (if none: write word + none)

9th Grade Word of The Day

Use the dictionary to write the definition and divide the words for each day below into syllables.

WEEK 28

MONDAY **WORD: Cellist**

TUESDAY **WORD: Coroner**

WEDNESDAY **WORD: Custodian**

THURSDAY **WORD: Cryptographer**

FRIDAY **WORD: Concierge**

SATURDAY / SUNDAY **WORD: Consul**

Write Words In ABC Order

For each word, find one synonym & one antonym. (if none: write word + none)

9th Grade Word of The Day

Use the dictionary to write the definition and divide the words for each day below into syllables.

WEEK 29

MONDAY **WORD: Dictator**

TUESDAY **WORD: Ecologist**

WEDNESDAY **WORD: Dermatologist**

THURSDAY **WORD: Economist**

FRIDAY **WORD: Entomologist**

SATURDAY / SUNDAY **WORD: Exterminator**

Write Words In ABC Order

For each word, find one synonym & one antonym. (if none: write word + none)

9th Grade Word of The Day

Use the dictionary to write the definition and divide the words for each day below into syllables.

WEEK 30

MONDAY **WORD: Emperor**

Write Words In ABC Order

TUESDAY **WORD: Falconer**

WEDNESDAY **WORD: Financier**

For each word, find one synonym & one antonym. (if none: write word + none)

THURSDAY **WORD: Flutist**

FRIDAY **WORD: Gemcutter**

SATURDAY / SUNDAY **WORD: Geneticist**

9th Grade Word of The Day

Use the dictionary to write the definition and divide the words for each day below into syllables.

WEEK 31

MONDAY **WORD: Linguist**

Write Words In ABC Order

TUESDAY **WORD: Librettist**

WEDNESDAY **WORD: Jester**

For each word, find one synonym & one antonym. (if none: write word + none)

THURSDAY **WORD: Laundress**

FRIDAY **WORD: Internist**

SATURDAY / SUNDAY **WORD: Harpist**

9th Grade Word of The Day

Use the dictionary to write the definition and divide the words for each day below into syllables.

WEEK 32

MONDAY **WORD: Lobbyist**

Write Words In ABC Order

TUESDAY **WORD: Muralist**

WEDNESDAY **WORD: Novelist**

For each word, find one synonym & one antonym. (if none: write word + none)

THURSDAY **WORD: Negotiator**

FRIDAY **WORD: Notary**

SATURDAY / SUNDAY **WORD: Oboist**

9th Grade Word of The Day

Use the dictionary to write the definition and divide the words for each day below into syllables.

WEEK 33

MONDAY **WORD: Peddler**

TUESDAY **WORD: Paleontologist**

WEDNESDAY **WORD: Oracle**

THURSDAY **WORD: Ophthalmologist**

FRIDAY **WORD: Ornithologist**

SATURDAY / SUNDAY **WORD: Optician**

Write Words In ABC Order

For each word, find one synonym & one antonym. (if none: write word + none)

9th Grade Word of The Day

Use the dictionary to write the definition and divide the words for each day below into syllables.

WEEK 34

MONDAY WORD: Philosopher
TUESDAY WORD: Psychologist
WEDNESDAY WORD: Pathologist
THURSDAY WORD: Pianist
FRIDAY WORD: Psychiatrist
SATURDAY / SUNDAY WORD: Paralegal
Write Words In ABC Order
For each word, find one synonym & one antonym. (if none: write word + none)

9th Grade Word of The Day

Use the dictionary to write the definition and divide the words for each day below into syllables.

WEEK 35

MONDAY **WORD: Pawnbroker**

TUESDAY **WORD: Percussionist**

WEDNESDAY **WORD: Philanthropist**

THURSDAY **WORD: Quilter**

FRIDAY **WORD: Radiologist**

SATURDAY / SUNDAY **WORD: Registrar**

Write Words In ABC Order

For each word, find one synonym & one antonym. (if none: write word + none)

9th Grade Word of The Day

Use the dictionary to write the definition and divide the words for each day below into syllables.

WEEK 36

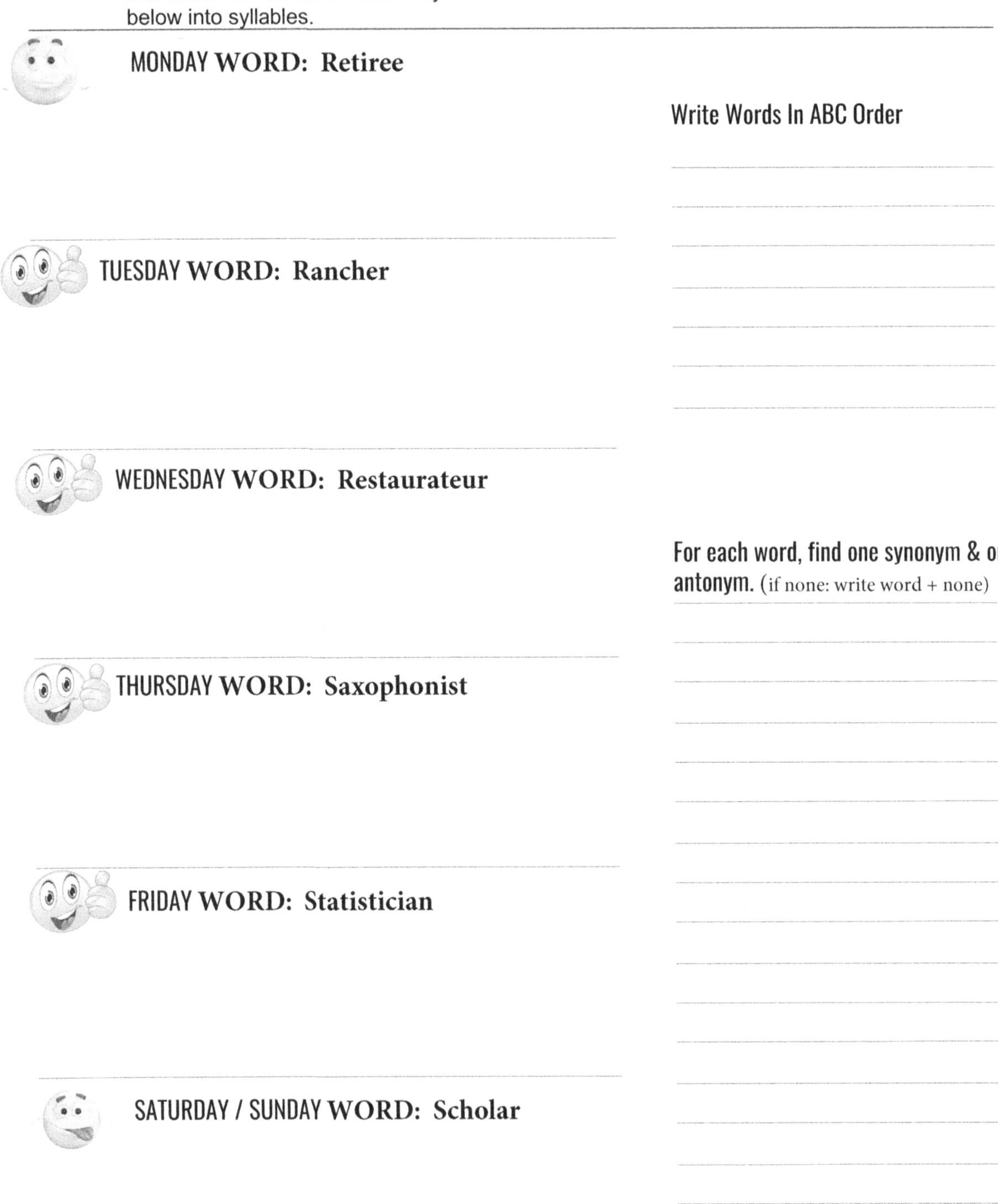

MONDAY WORD: Retiree
Write Words In ABC Order
TUESDAY WORD: Rancher
WEDNESDAY WORD: Restaurateur
For each word, find one synonym & one antonym. (if none: write word + none)
THURSDAY WORD: Saxophonist
FRIDAY WORD: Statistician
SATURDAY / SUNDAY WORD: Scholar

9th Grade Word of The Day

Use the dictionary to write the definition and divide the words for each day below into syllables.

WEEK 37

MONDAY **WORD: Stockbroker**

TUESDAY **WORD: Samurai**

WEDNESDAY **WORD: Seamstress**

THURSDAY **WORD: Socialite**

FRIDAY **WORD: Surveyor**

SATURDAY / SUNDAY **WORD: Taxidermist**

Write Words In ABC Order

For each word, find one synonym & one antonym. (if none: write word + none)

9th Grade Word of The Day

Use the dictionary to write the definition and divide the words for each day below into syllables.

WEEK 38

MONDAY **WORD: Treasurer**

Write Words In ABC Order

TUESDAY **WORD: Typist**

WEDNESDAY **WORD: Tiler**

For each word, find one synonym & one antonym. (if none: write word + none)

THURSDAY **WORD: Umpire**

FRIDAY **WORD: Vicar**

SATURDAY / SUNDAY **WORD: Violinist**

9th Grade Word of The Day

Use the dictionary to write the definition and divide the words for each day below into syllables.

People: WEEK 39

MONDAY **WORD: Amigo**

TUESDAY **WORD: Antagonist**

WEDNESDAY **WORD: Apparition**

THURSDAY **WORD: Adversary**

FRIDAY **WORD: Adolescent**

SATURDAY / SUNDAY **WORD: Ally**

Write Words In ABC Order

For each word, find one synonym & one antonym. (if none: write word + none)

9th Grade Word of The Day

Use the dictionary to write the definition and divide the words for each day below into syllables.

WEEK 40

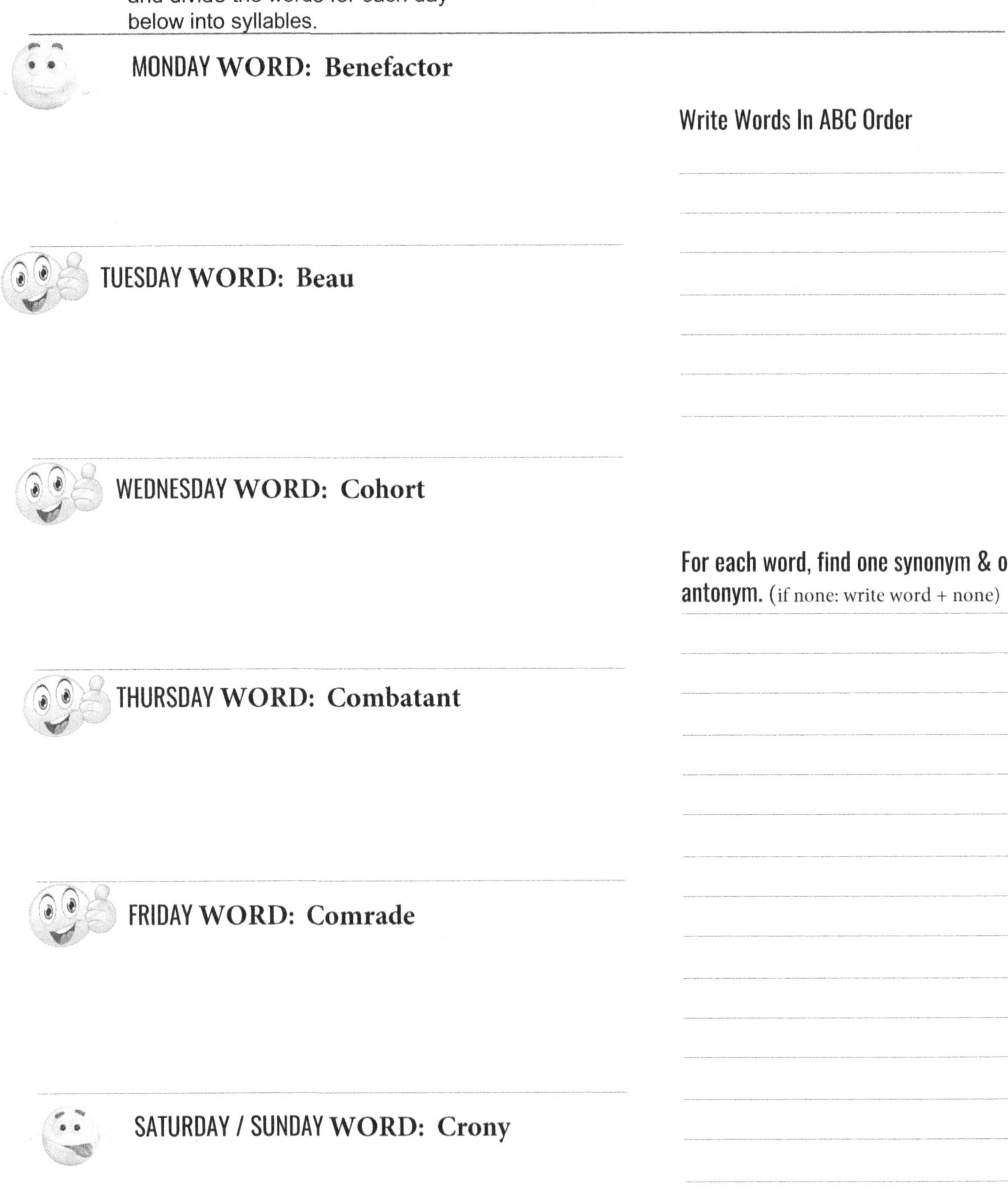

MONDAY **WORD: Benefactor**

Write Words In ABC Order

TUESDAY **WORD: Beau**

WEDNESDAY **WORD: Cohort**

For each word, find one synonym & one antonym. (if none: write word + none)

THURSDAY **WORD: Combatant**

FRIDAY **WORD: Comrade**

SATURDAY / SUNDAY **WORD: Crony**

9th Grade Word of The Day

Use the dictionary to write the definition and divide the words for each day below into syllables.

WEEK 41

MONDAY **WORD: Collaborator**

TUESDAY **WORD: Compadre**

WEDNESDAY **WORD: Cherub**

THURSDAY **WORD: Chum**

FRIDAY **WORD: Confidant**

SATURDAY / SUNDAY **WORD: Descendant**

Write Words In ABC Order

For each word, find one synonym & one antonym. (if none: write word + none)

9th Grade Word of The Day

Use the dictionary to write the definition and divide the words for each day below into syllables.

WEEK 42

MONDAY **WORD: Doppelgänger**

TUESDAY **WORD: Fiancée**

WEDNESDAY **WORD: Flatmate**

THURSDAY **WORD: Fiancé**

FRIDAY **WORD: Foe**

SATURDAY / SUNDAY **WORD: Inhabitant**

Write Words In ABC Order

For each word, find one synonym & one antonym. (if none: write word + none)

9th Grade Word of The Day

Use the dictionary to write the definition and divide the words for each day below into syllables.

WEEK 43

MONDAY **WORD: Lassie**

TUESDAY **WORD: Laddie**

WEDNESDAY **WORD: Populace**

THURSDAY **WORD: Sophomore**

FRIDAY **WORD: Socialite**

SATURDAY / SUNDAY **WORD: Tween**

Write Words In ABC Order

For each word, find one synonym & one antonym. (if none: write word + none)

9th Grade Word of The Day

Use the dictionary to write the definition and divide the words for each day below into syllables.

Good Luck: WEEK 44

MONDAY **WORD: Amulets**

Write Words In ABC Order

TUESDAY **WORD: Ankh**

WEDNESDAY **WORD: Bamboo**

For each word, find one synonym & one antonym. (if none: write word + none)

THURSDAY **WORD: Dreamcatcher**

FRIDAY **WORD: Wishbones**

SATURDAY / SUNDAY **WORD: Scarab Beetles**

9th Grade Word of The Day

Use the dictionary to write the definition and divide the words for each day below into syllables.

Emotions: WEEK 45

MONDAY **WORD: Assertive**

TUESDAY **WORD: Agitation**

WEDNESDAY **WORD: Anguish**

THURSDAY **WORD: Adoration**

FRIDAY **WORD: Alienation**

SATURDAY / SUNDAY **WORD: Apprehension**

Write Words In ABC Order

For each word, find one synonym & one antonym. (if none: write word + none)

9th Grade Word of The Day

Use the dictionary to write the definition and divide the words for each day below into syllables.

WEEK 46

MONDAY WORD: **Beleaguered**

TUESDAY WORD: **Bliss**

WEDNESDAY WORD: **Bewitched**

THURSDAY WORD: **Complacent**

FRIDAY WORD: **Conceited**

SATURDAY / SUNDAY WORD: **Compliant**

Write Words In ABC Order

For each word, find one synonym & one antonym. (if none: write word + none)

9th Grade Word of The Day

Use the dictionary to write the definition and divide the words for each day below into syllables.

WEEK 47

MONDAY **WORD: Contentment**

TUESDAY **WORD: Capricious**

WEDNESDAY **WORD: Disenchanted**

THURSDAY **WORD: Defiance**

FRIDAY **WORD: Disillusioned**

SATURDAY / SUNDAY **WORD: Enamored**

Write Words In ABC Order

For each word, find one synonym & one antonym. (if none: write word + none)

9th Grade Word of The Day

Use the dictionary to write the definition and divide the words for each day below into syllables.

WEEK 48

MONDAY WORD: **Equanimity**

TUESDAY WORD: **Exuberant**

WEDNESDAY WORD: **Enraptured**

THURSDAY WORD: **Euphoria**

FRIDAY WORD: **Enthralled**

SATURDAY / SUNDAY WORD: **Exasperation**

Write Words In ABC Order

For each word, find one synonym & one antonym. (if none: write word + none)

9th Grade Word of The Day

Use the dictionary to write the definition and divide the words for each day below into syllables.

WEEK 49

MONDAY **WORD: Fatalistic**

TUESDAY **WORD: Ferocity**

WEDNESDAY **WORD: Flummoxed**

THURSDAY **WORD: Glum**

FRIDAY **WORD: Hysteria**

SATURDAY / SUNDAY **WORD: Introverted**

Write Words In ABC Order

For each word, find one synonym & one antonym. (if none: write word + none)

9th Grade Word of The Day

Use the dictionary to write the definition and divide the words for each day below into syllables.

WEEK 50

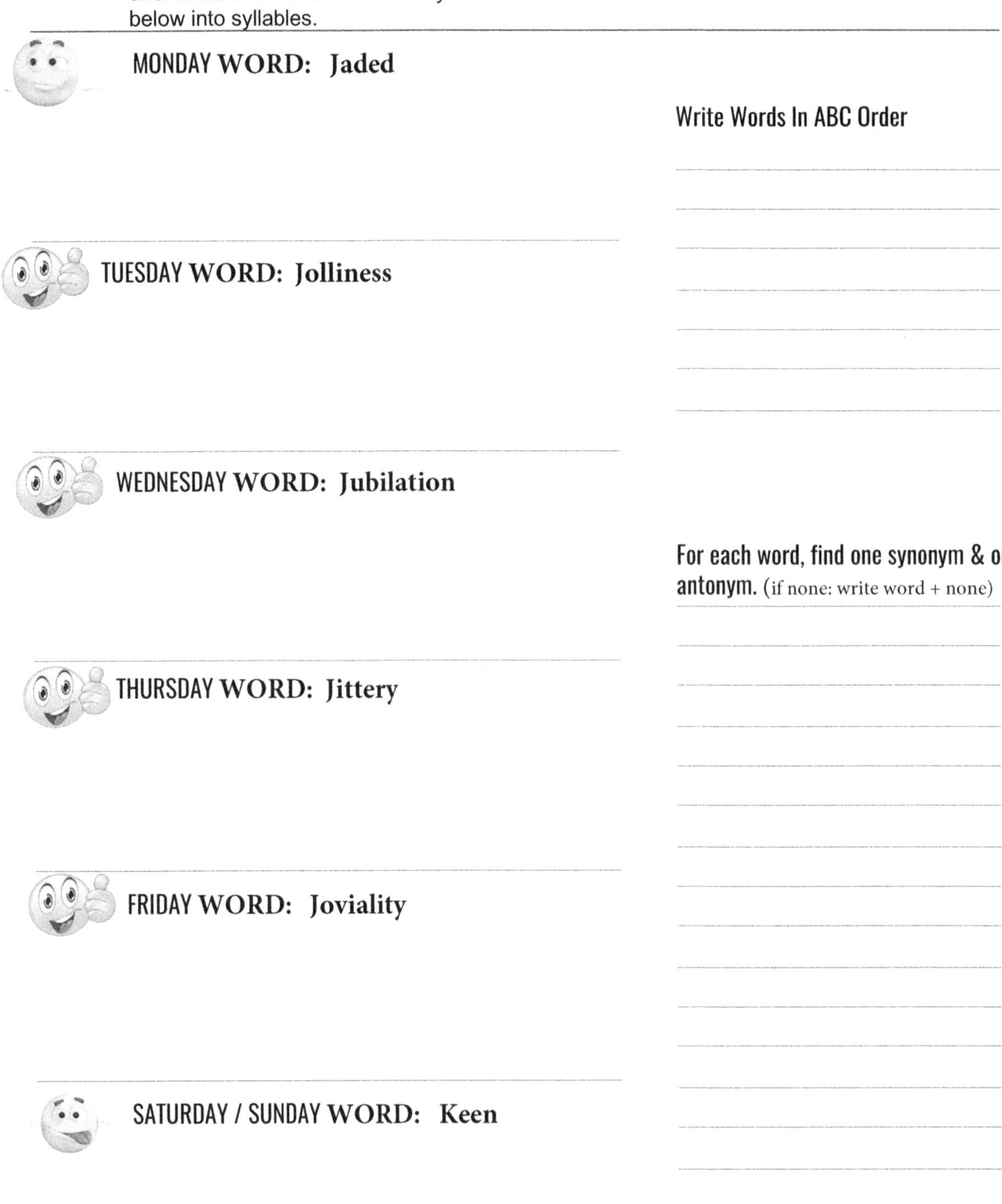

MONDAY WORD: Jaded
TUESDAY WORD: Jolliness
WEDNESDAY WORD: Jubilation
THURSDAY WORD: Jittery
FRIDAY WORD: Joviality
SATURDAY / SUNDAY WORD: Keen
Write Words In ABC Order
For each word, find one synonym & one antonym. (if none: write word + none)

9th Grade Word of The Day

Use the dictionary to write the definition and divide the words for each day below into syllables.

WEEK 51

MONDAY **WORD: Lulled**

TUESDAY **WORD: Loathing**

WEDNESDAY **WORD: Modesty**

THURSDAY **WORD: Mortification**

FRIDAY **WORD: Nirvana**

SATURDAY / SUNDAY **WORD: Optimism**

Write Words In ABC Order

For each word, find one synonym & one antonym. (if none: write word + none)

9th Grade Word of The Day

Use the dictionary to write the definition and divide the words for each day below into syllables.

WEEK 52

MONDAY **WORD: Ornery**

TUESDAY **WORD: Pensive**

WEDNESDAY **WORD: Placid**

THURSDAY **WORD: Pessimism**

FRIDAY **WORD: Quarrelsome**

SATURDAY / SUNDAY **WORD: Querulous**

Write Words In ABC Order

For each word, find one synonym & one antonym. (if none: write word + none)

9th Grade Word of The Day

Use the dictionary to write the definition and divide the words for each day below into syllables.

WEEK 53

MONDAY **WORD: Sardonic**

TUESDAY **WORD: Repentance**

WEDNESDAY **WORD: Revulsion**

THURSDAY **WORD: Resentment**

FRIDAY **WORD: Roused**

SATURDAY / SUNDAY **WORD: Remorse**

Write Words In ABC Order

For each word, find one synonym & one antonym. (if none: write word + none)

9th Grade Word of The Day

Use the dictionary to write the definition and divide the words for each day below into syllables.

WEEK 54

MONDAY **WORD: Sentimentality**

Write Words In ABC Order

TUESDAY **WORD: Scorn**

WEDNESDAY **WORD: Stoical**

For each word, find one synonym & one antonym. (if none: write word + none)

THURSDAY **WORD: Subdued**

FRIDAY **WORD: Timidity**

SATURDAY / SUNDAY **WORD: Tranquil**

9th Grade Word of The Day

Use the dictionary to write the definition and divide the words for each day below into syllables.

WEEK 55

MONDAY **WORD: Vengeful**

TUESDAY **WORD: Triumphant**

WEDNESDAY **WORD: Vain**

THURSDAY **WORD: Wrathful**

FRIDAY **WORD: Vigilance**

SATURDAY / SUNDAY **WORD: Zeal**

Write Words In ABC Order

For each word, find one synonym & one antonym. (if none: write word + none)

9th Grade Word of The Day

Use the dictionary to write the definition and divide the words for each day below into syllables.

Math: WEEK 56

MONDAY **WORD: Equilateral**

Write Words In ABC Order

TUESDAY **WORD: Factorial**

WEDNESDAY **WORD: Cosine**

For each word, find one synonym & one antonym. (if none: write word + none)

THURSDAY **WORD: Perpendicular**

FRIDAY **WORD: Hypotenuse**

SATURDAY / SUNDAY **WORD: Multiplicand**

9th Grade Word of The Day

Use the dictionary to write the definition and divide the words for each day below into syllables.

Rocks And Minerals
WEEK 57

MONDAY WORD: **Aquamarine**

TUESDAY WORD: **Azurite**

WEDNESDAY WORD: **Basalt**

THURSDAY WORD: **Beryl**

FRIDAY WORD: **Alexandrite**

SATURDAY / SUNDAY WORD: **Aventurine**

Write Words In ABC Order

For each word, find one synonym & one antonym. (if none: write word + none)

9th Grade Word of The Day

Use the dictionary to write the definition and divide the words for each day below into syllables.

WEEK 58

MONDAY WORD: **Chalcedony**

Write Words In ABC Order

TUESDAY WORD: **Citrine**

WEDNESDAY WORD: **Dolomite**

For each word, find one synonym & one antonym. (if none: write word + none)

THURSDAY WORD: **Calcite**

FRIDAY WORD: **Carnelian**

SATURDAY / SUNDAY WORD: **Druze**

9th Grade Word of The Day

Use the dictionary to write the definition and divide the words for each day below into syllables.

WEEK 59

MONDAY **WORD: Facet**

TUESDAY **WORD: Geode**

WEDNESDAY **WORD: Feldspar**

THURSDAY **WORD: Granite**

FRIDAY **WORD: Gneiss**

SATURDAY / SUNDAY **WORD: Fluorite**

Write Words In ABC Order

For each word, find one synonym & one antonym. (if none: write word + none)

9th Grade Word of The Day

Use the dictionary to write the definition and divide the words for each day below into syllables.

WEEK 60

MONDAY **WORD: Hematite**

TUESDAY **WORD: Gypsum**

WEDNESDAY **WORD: Howlite**

THURSDAY **WORD: Jadeite**

FRIDAY **WORD: Igneous Rock**

SATURDAY / SUNDAY **WORD: Jasper**

Write Words In ABC Order

For each word, find one synonym & one antonym. (if none: write word + none)

9th Grade Word of The Day

Use the dictionary to write the definition and divide the words for each day below into syllables.

WEEK 61

MONDAY **WORD: Lapidary**

Write Words In ABC Order

TUESDAY **WORD: Labradorite**

WEDNESDAY **WORD: Loess**

For each word, find one synonym & one antonym. (if none: write word + none)

THURSDAY **WORD: Kunzite**

FRIDAY **WORD: Limestone**

SATURDAY / SUNDAY **WORD: Lithified**

9th Grade Word of The Day

Use the dictionary to write the definition and divide the words for each day below into syllables.

The Constitution: **WEEK 62**

MONDAY **WORD: Allegiance**

Write Words In ABC Order

TUESDAY **WORD: Amendment**

WEDNESDAY **WORD: Democracy**

For each word, find one synonym & one antonym. (if none: write word + none)

THURSDAY **WORD: Executive Branch**

FRIDAY **WORD: Electoral College**

SATURDAY / SUNDAY **WORD: Bicameral**

9th Grade Word of The Day

Use the dictionary to write the definition and divide the words for each day below into syllables.

WEEK 63

MONDAY **WORD: Impeachment**

Write Words In ABC Order

TUESDAY **WORD: Magna Carta**

WEDNESDAY **WORD: Monarchy**

For each word, find one synonym & one antonym. (if none: write word + none)

THURSDAY **WORD: Ratification**

FRIDAY **WORD: Succession**

SATURDAY / SUNDAY **WORD: Senatorial**

9th Grade Word of The Day

Use the dictionary to write the definition and divide the words for each day below into syllables.

Measurement: **WEEK 64**

MONDAY **WORD: Angstrom**

Write Words In ABC Order

TUESDAY **WORD: Breadth**

WEDNESDAY **WORD: Carat**

For each word, find one synonym & one antonym. (if none: write word + none)

THURSDAY **WORD: Bushel**

FRIDAY **WORD: Byte**

SATURDAY / SUNDAY **WORD: Bale**

9th Grade Word of The Day

Use the dictionary to write the definition and divide the words for each day below into syllables.

WEEK 65

MONDAY **WORD: Deciliter**

Write Words In ABC Order

TUESDAY **WORD: Fathom**

WEDNESDAY **WORD: Dram**

For each word, find one synonym & one antonym. (if none: write word + none)

THURSDAY **WORD: Folio**

FRIDAY **WORD: Furlong**

SATURDAY / SUNDAY **WORD: Dry Quart**

9th Grade Word of The Day

Use the dictionary to write the definition and divide the words for each day below into syllables.

WEEK 66

MONDAY WORD: Fermi
TUESDAY WORD: Hectare
WEDNESDAY WORD: Microliter
THURSDAY WORD: Nautical Mile
FRIDAY WORD: Megaparsec
SATURDAY / SUNDAY WORD: Nanometer

Write Words In ABC Order

For each word, find one synonym & one antonym. (if none: write word + none)

9th Grade Word of The Day

Use the dictionary to write the definition and divide the words for each day below into syllables.

WEEK 67

MONDAY **WORD: Octant**

TUESDAY **WORD: Octave**

WEDNESDAY **WORD: Picoliter**

THURSDAY **WORD: Picogram**

FRIDAY **WORD: Octad**

SATURDAY / SUNDAY **WORD: Picometer**

Write Words In ABC Order

For each word, find one synonym & one antonym. (if none: write word + none)

9th Grade Word of The Day

Use the dictionary to write the definition and divide the words for each day below into syllables.

WEEK 68

MONDAY **WORD: Quadrant**

Write Words In ABC Order

TUESDAY **WORD: Ream**

WEDNESDAY **WORD: Quartile**

For each word, find one synonym & one antonym. (if none: write word + none)

THURSDAY **WORD: Sheaf**

FRIDAY **WORD: Radian**

SATURDAY / SUNDAY **WORD: Smoot**

9th Grade Word of The Day

Use the dictionary to write the definition and divide the words for each day below into syllables.

WEEK 69

MONDAY **WORD: Skein**

TUESDAY **WORD: Stade**

WEDNESDAY **WORD: Troy Pound**

THURSDAY **WORD: Yardstick**

FRIDAY **WORD: Smidgen**

SATURDAY / SUNDAY **WORD: Zoll**

Write Words In ABC Order

For each word, find one synonym & one antonym. (if none: write word + none)

9th Grade Word of The Day

Use the dictionary to write the definition and divide the words for each day below into syllables.

Geography: WEEK 70

MONDAY **WORD: Analemma**

Write Words In ABC Order

TUESDAY **WORD: Azimuth**

WEDNESDAY **WORD: Cartography**

For each word, find one synonym & one antonym. (if none: write word + none)

THURSDAY **WORD: Bathymetric Map**

FRIDAY **WORD: Meridian**

SATURDAY / SUNDAY **WORD: Hemisphere**

9th Grade Word of The Day

Use the dictionary to write the definition and divide the words for each day below into syllables.

WEEK 71

MONDAY **WORD: Mercator Projection**

TUESDAY **WORD: Nautical Chart**

WEDNESDAY **WORD: Peak**

THURSDAY **WORD: Relief Map**

FRIDAY **WORD: Prime Meridian**

SATURDAY / SUNDAY **WORD: Topography**

Write Words In ABC Order

For each word, find one synonym & one antonym. (if none: write word + none)

Score: ____________

Quantitative Chemistry

Date: __________

		A	B	C	D
1.	____________	Forrmula	Formula	Formola	Forrmola
2.	____________	Isutope	Iscotope	Issotope	Isotope
3.	____________	Neottron	Neuttron	Neotron	Neutron
4.	____________	Prruton	Prroton	Proton	Pruton
5.	____________	Mole	Molle	Mzle	Mulle
6.	____________	Ellectron	Electrun	Ellectrun	Electron
7.	____________	Compound	Compoud	Compood	Compoond
8.	____________	Ellenment	Element	Elenment	Ellement
9.	____________	Percentadge	Percentage	Perrcentadge	Perrcentage
10.	____________	Divission	Divissoin	Divisoin	Division
11.	____________	Equattoin	Equation	Equatoin	Equattion
12.	____________	Abundane	Abrundane	Abundence	Abundance
13.	____________	Rellative	Rellatave	Relative	Relatave
14.	____________	Noclleus	Nucleus	Nocleus	Nuclleus
15.	____________	Charrge	Charrje	Charge	Charje

Write sentences using as many of the words above in a single sentence. Use your book to help you.

1. ____________

2. ____________

3. ____________

4. ____________

5. ____________

Score: ______________________

Adding Ending to Words

Date: __________

Place the letter of the column that contains the correctly spelled word in the blank.

		A	B	C	D
1.	________	nulified	nulifeid	nullified	nullifeid
2.	________	separatang	separating	separrating	separratang
3.	________	harrvesting	harrvestang	harvesting	harvestang
4.	________	conttianed	contained	conttained	contianed
5.	________	prugramming	programing	prugraming	programming
6.	________	reffuced	reffused	refused	refuced
7.	________	omated	omatted	omited	omitted
8.	________	produced	prrodused	prodused	prroduced
9.	________	acquired	acqoirred	acquirred	acqoired
10.	________	abillities	abiliteis	abilliteis	abilities
11.	________	submitted	submited	sobmitted	sobmited
12.	________	jusstified	justified	jusstifeid	justifeid
13.	________	forbiding	furbidding	furbiding	forbidding
14.	________	pettrifeid	pettrified	petrified	petrifeid
15.	________	nutrients	nuttrients	nutreints	nuttreints
16.	________	resources	ressources	resoorces	ressoorces
17.	________	judicious	judicoiuss	judicoius	judiciouss
18.	________	category	categury	cattegory	cattegury
19.	________	cemettery	cametery	camettery	cemetery
20.	________	indelible	indelable	indellable	indellible

Score: ____________

Spelling 9th Grade

Date: ____________

	A	B	C	D
1.	reactoin	reacttion	reaction	reacttoin
2.	prerecurded	prrerecurded	prrerecorded	prerecorded
3.	incurectly	incorectly	incurrectly	incorrectly
4.	incredibly	incredably	incrredibly	incrredably
5.	dissobedeint	disobedient	disobedeint	dissobedient
6.	disagreeable	disagreable	disagraeble	disagreaeble
7.	declaratoin	declaration	decllaratoin	decllaration
8.	quesstoinable	questoinable	quesstionable	questionable
9.	repaymentt	repeymentt	repeyment	repayment
10.	reffreshment	refreshment	refreshnment	reffreshnment
11.	unbrraekable	unbraekable	unbreakable	unbrreakable
12.	spurrtsmanship	sporrtsmanship	spurtsmanship	sportsmanship
13.	glefully	gleafully	glephully	gleefully
14.	rettirenment	retirenment	retirement	rettirement
15.	watchfuly	watchphully	watchphuly	watchfully
16.	missdailed	misdialed	misdailed	missdialed
17.	undephined	undeffined	undephfined	undefined
18.	dissplacenment	dissplacement	displacement	displacenment
19.	madshipman	midsshipman	midschipman	midshipman
20.	unhapily	unhapaly	unhappily	unhappaly
21.	multicultural	mollticultural	molticultural	mullticultural
22.	universally	universaly	unaversally	unaversaly
23.	understatenment	underrstatement	underrstatenment	understatement
24.	ootlandish	outlandish	outtlandish	oottlandish
25.	imflamible	imflamable	imflammable	imflammible

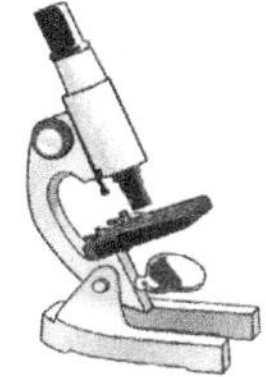

Cell Theory

Score: ____________________

Date: ____________

Read through the passage and place the correct words in the spaces.

prove	changed	tissue	plant	blocks
human	building	microscopes	discoloured	conclusion
tiniest	differences	technology	Schwann	originated
cell	division'	theory	cloudy	parts
pre-existing	organism	scientists	cartilage	animal
open	Pasteur	process	develop	spontaneous
build	nucleus			

______________ studied __________ and animal cells under a microscope. He could see that both types of cell had a nucleus and other cell structures that were the same.

Schleiden studied plant and ____________ cells too. He also saw that the plant and animal cells had the same ________ structures. Animal cells from different ____________ around the body were found to have ______________________, but they still had a ______________ in their structure.

Schwann and Schleiden both came to the ____________________ that cells were the basic ________________ ____________ of all life, but they did not agree on how cells ____________________. Schleiden believed that cells originated through ' ______________________ generation '. Schwann believed that cells originated from ________________________ cells. He also believed that cells, once generated, could ______________ in different ways to form different __________ of a living ________________, like cheek cells, skin or __________________ in a __________ body. The process of cells originating from other cells is called 'cell __________________.

About 20 years later, ______________ put soup in two different flasks. One was open and the other had an s-shaped neck. The broth in the container that was left ________ changed over time and became

________________________ and ____________. Pasteur said that if 'spontaneous generation' was a real

_______________, both containers of broth would have _______________.

As _____________________ has progressed, _____________________ have had better ________________________

so that they could research more about cells and cell ____________. Over time scientists have been able to

__________ the theories of scientists like Schwann and Pasteur correct, and they have been able to

__________ on the knowledge of cell theory. Microscopes now can see the tiniest structures in the

_______________ cells, and scientists now know a lot more about how cells originate, and how they work and

form into different types of cells.

Eighth Grade Vocabulary Quiz

Score: ______________

Date: __________

Match the letter to the correct term.

1	☐	avert -	- characterized by being boring and always the same way; dull, tedious, and repetitious; without variety and interest	A
2	☐	belligerent -	- to get control of someone or something that is violent or dangerous by using force; to get control over something strong such as an emotion	B
3	☐	cower -	- to give payback; to return a hurt that someone has caused you; to answer or respond to an argument with a counter argument	C
4	☐	crafty -	- clever typically in a deceptive or dishonest way; skillful in using subtle and/or unique ways to trick someone	D
5	☐	indignation -	- to be angry and upset about something and to refuse to discuss it with other people; to be quiet and moody	E
6	☐	monotonous -	- angry and aggressive; feeling or showing readiness to fight	F
7	☐	retort -	- anger caused by something unjust, unworthy, or mean	G
8	☐	subdue -	- a feeling of great pain or sadness; a condition of deep suffering from misfortune, affliction, or grief	H
9	☐	sulk -	- to move back or bend downward out of fear of something approaching; to shrink away or crouch for shelter from harm	I
10	☐	woe -	- to turn away or aside (such as the eyes) in order to avoid; to prevent something bad from happening	J

Eighth Grade Vocabulary Quiz

Score: ____________________

Date: ____________

Match the letter to the correct term.

1	☐	complacent -	- satisfied with how things are and against change; satisfied and often unaware of danger or deficiency	A
2	☐	dejected -	- to put to death usually by hanging without a public trial or conviction of guilt--often carried out by a mob or angry group of citizens	B
3	☐	deride -	- having or showing the proud and unkind attitude of someone who gives orders and expects others to obey them immediately	C
4	☐	imperious -	- having or expressing doubt about something; not easily convinced; having doubts or reservations	D
5	☐	juncture -	- to talk or write about someone or something in a very critical or insulting way	E
6	☐	lynch -	- showing a lot of deep and earnest respect	F
7	☐	morose -	- sad because of a failure or loss	G
8	☐	mottled -	- sad or unhappy; having a sullen and gloomy mood or disposition	H
9	☐	reverent -	- marked with spots or spears of color	I
10	☐	skeptical -	- a place where things meet and join together; an important or critical point in time when a decision is made or actions taken	J

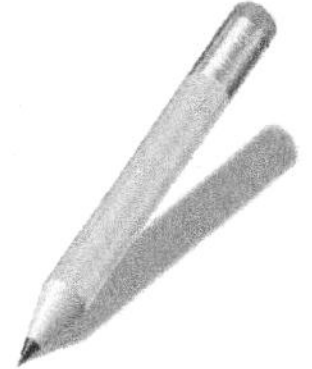

Materials Technology

Score: ______________

Date: __________

Use the letters on each line and unscramble the letters make a word in Technology.

round	buckle	irregular	drying	classified	milling
fibreboard	wood	logging	softwood	harvested	timber
specifically	Balsa	plywood	structure	natural	construction
seasoning	manufactured	undesirable	particleboard	storage	cutting
hardwood	rectangular				

1. lgiggon l _ _ _ _ _ _
2. yoldwop p _ _ _ _ _ _
3. clorrptaebdai p _ _ _ _ _ _ _ _ _ _ _ _
4. bdaeorbifr f _ _ _ _ _ _ _ _ _
5. mncurdfeatau m _ _ _ _ _ _ _ _ _ _ _
6. rwdoaohd h _ _ _ _ _ _ _
7. tosdwoof s _ _ _ _ _ _ _
8. liigmnl m _ _ _ _ _ _
9. isnagoens s _ _ _ _ _ _ _ _
10. mebtir t _ _ _ _ _
11. dniryg d _ _ _ _ _
12. trtruucse s _ _ _ _ _ _ _ _
13. ntaaurl n _ _ _ _ _ _
14. heasedtvr h _ _ _ _ _ _ _ _
15. iosrocnnctut c _ _ _ _ _ _ _ _ _ _ _
16. eblcuk b _ _ _ _ _
17. tcnutgi c _ _ _ _ _ _
18. iaylscfcepil s _ _ _ _ _ _ _ _ _ _ _

19. edlirunsaeb u _ _ _ _ _ _ _ _ _ _

20. doow w _ _ _

21. riaeurglr i _ _ _ _ _ _ _ _

22. gstaoer s _ _ _ _ _ _

23. difisselac c _ _ _ _ _ _ _ _ _

24. alabs B _ _ _ _

25. aartcurengl r _ _ _ _ _ _ _ _ _ _

26. rdonu r _ _ _ _

Write sentences using words from above:

1. ______

2. ______

3. ______

4. ______

5. ______

6. ______

7. ______

8. ______

9. ______

10. ______

Score: ____________________

9th Grade Spelling

Date: ____________

fill in the blank with the missing letters

undergo	overdrive	overreact	overheat	submarine	overestimate
subcommittee	underscore	underdeveloped	undreline	overboard	underbrush
subartic	overlook	overpass	overwhelmed	undertow	subway
Overactive	underwater	overhand	overbite	overact	

1. rvaviceteo _ v _ _ _ c _ i _ _

2. verbteoi _ _ _ r _ _ _ e

3. boorvdera o v _ _ _ _ _ _ _

4. vtmeeeaiosrt _ v _ _ _ _ _ _ _ _ t e

5. drovaehn _ _ e _ h _ _ _

6. areteorvc _ _ _ _ _ _ e _ _ t

7. lrddvenuepeedo _ _ d e _ d _ _ _ _ _ p _ _

8. onerdug u _ _ e _ _ _

9. rcesnerodu _ n _ _ r s _ _ _ _

10. eeiudnrnl _ n _ _ _ _ _ n _

11. uhrersudnb u _ _ _ _ _ _ _ s h

12. etmsbecotmiu s _ _ c _ _ _ i _ _ _ _

13. ubnsiream _ _ _ _ _ _ i n _

14. ywaubs _ _ _ w a _

15. vdewromhele _ _ e r _ h _ _ _ _ _

16. csbatrui _ u _ _ _ _ i _

17. ouentwdr _ _ _ e r _ _ _

18. okerovlo _ v _ _ _ _ _ k

19. oacvetr o _ e _ _ _ _

20. auretwednr _ _ d e _ w _ _ _ _
21. evirdvroe _ _ e _ _ r _ _ _
22. erhteova _ _ _ _ _ e a _
23. ovpaesrs o _ _ _ _ _ _ s

Score: ____________________

9th Grade Vocabulary

Date: ____________

Circle the correct vocabulary word that best fits the definition or fills in the blank.

1. The wildfire __________ the forest until there was nothing left.

a. scorched

b. showered

c. condemned

2. A time of unusually dry weather and no rain

a. phase

b. drought

c. period

3. When my dogs_______ a bad smell, I know it's time to give them a bath.

a. fume

b. smell

c. emit

4. _______ is is dish made from beans.

a. Frijoles

b. Legumes

c. Squash

5. Broken pieces created when a building is destroyed

a. rubble

b. gravel

c. junk

6. A helper in schools and hospitals

a. gofer

b. auxiliary

c. aide

7. Use of teasing to be funny, mean, or hurtful

a. sincere

b. sarcasm

c. scorn

8. Things that limit a person's physical and mental abilities

a. determination

b. courage

c. disabilities

9. A different or new form of something

a. version

b. deal

c. object

10. Hot, glowing remains of a fire

a. twiglets

b. embers

c. wood

11. To save something from being wasted

a. prepare

b. confine

c. conserve

12. Following a recipe is an _______ way to cook a delicious dish.

a. prompt

b. effective

c. clean

13. abuela (ah-BWEH-lah)

a. grandmother

b. sister

c. brother

14. Aria spent her Saturday __________ through a park.

a. roaming

b. climbing

c. shuffling

15. To light on fire

a. ignite

b. start

c. snare

RESPIRATORY SYSTEM

Score: ______________________

Date: ______________

FILL IN THE BLANK WITH THE BEST ANSWER.

pneumonia	dyspnea	empyema	Atelectasis	Asthma
tachypneic	apnea	Olfaction	Tidal	pnea
py/o	ABG's	nas/o	epiglottis	bronchoscope
CO2	residual	hemoptysis	influenza	rhinoplasty
mediastinum	epistaxis	orthopnea	cheyne-stokes	pleurisy
diaphragm	cyanotic	Pulmonary	eu	thoracentesis
Rhonchi	Inhalation	rale	alveoli	emphysema
sputum	trachea	thyroid	Asthma	pulmon/o

1. The ______________________ is the space in the central portion of the thoracic cavity, between the lungs.
2. The ______________ are the air sacs of the lungs where O2 and CO2 are exchanged.
3. The medical term for nosebleed is __________________.
4. Mr. Jones' mucous membranes appeared to be bluish or grayish or ________________.
5. ____________ is a lung disease characterized by wheezing, dyspnea, and a feeling of chest or airway constriction,
6. ____________________ is the process of breathing air into the lungs.
7. A rhythmic cycle of breathing with an increase in respiration followed by apnea is called __________________________ respiration.
8. A chronic pulmonary disease in which it is difficult to exhale air from the lungs is called __________________.
9. The inability to breathe unless in an upright position is called __________________.
10. ______________________ is imperfect dilation of the lungs, collapse of an alveolus, a lobule or a lung.
11. The condition of spitting up blood is called ____________________.
12. The breath sound ______________ means "snore".
13. After breaking his nose, Joe was scheduled for ______________________ or surgical repair.
14. In the term pyothorax, the combining form ________ means pus.

15. Periods of temporary cessation of breathing is called __________.

16. __________________ function tests are series of tests to determine the diffusion of O2 and CO2 across the cell membrane in the lungs.

17. The pulmonologist will use a _________________________ to visually examine the larynx, trachea, and bronchi.

18. The ____________________ acts as a lid to prevent aspiration of food into the trachea.

19. Mrs. Kay was having episodes of ______________ or difficult breathing post-op.

20. During an anxiety attack, Mindy was ____________________ or breathing fast.

21. H3N2 or __________________ is an ACUTE contagious respiratory infection caused by a virus.

22. After receiving respiratory treatments for a severe respiratory infection, Mrs. Johnson was able to cough up a significant amount of ____________.

23. __________________ is the process of smelling.

24. In determining respiratory acidosis/alkalosis or metabolic acidosis/alkalosis, Arterial Blood Gases or __________ are vital.

25. A surgical puncture of the chest to remove fluid in called a ___________________________.

26. The physician reported to Mr. Noon that his chest x-ray showed he had __________________ or inflammation of the lung.

27. __________ volume is the amount of air in a single inspiration or exhalation.

28. The __________________ is a musculomembranous wall that separates the thoracic and abdominal cavities.

29. Pus located in the pleural cavity is aka ______________.

30. Inflammation of the pleura or lining of the lung is called ________________.

31. The prefix ____- in eupnea means good or normal. As in good or normal breathing.

32. Located in the larynx, the ______________ cartilage or adam's apple is the largest cartilage in that structure.

33. The words part for nose are __________ or rhin/o.

34. The right and left bronchus are two main branches of the ______________.

35. The word part for breathing is -________.

36. ____________ is an inflammatory disease of the bronchi characterized by wheezing, dyspnea and constriction of the chest.

37. The ________________ volume is the amount of air remaining in the lungs after maximal exhalation.

38. This breath sound called a ________, is a crackling or rattling sound heard in the chest.

39. The word parts pulm/o or ________________ means lung.

40. The respiratory system's primary function is to furnish O2 and to remove ______ from the cells and tissues.

Central and Southern Asia

Score: ____________________

Date: ____________

Fill in the blanks with words from the box.

Ganges	Himalayan	Mumbai	Caste	Delhi
China	900	untouchable	warmest	Nepal
Indian	Indus	4	triangle	Everest

There are three valleys in Central and Southern Asia: The _______________ Valley, The Tigris/Euphrates Valley, and the Huang He Valley.

India is a peninsula which looks like an upside down _______________. On the Western shore of India lies the _______________ Ocean. It is the _______________ ocean of all. This is mainly because the Gulf Stream passes through.

Along the western shore of India, there are two port cities. One is the large, modern city of _______________ (Bombay). The other is another large city called Calcutta. The capital of India is New _______________.

To the north, the _______________ Mountains provide a natural barrier between India and _______________. The world's tallest mountain, Mt. _______________, is in the Himalayas. It lies in the small country of _______________ which lies to the northeast of India.

There are three main rivers in India. They are the Indus River, the _______________ River and the Brahmaputra River. The Indus river flows _______________ miles from the base of the Himalayas to the coast.

The Indian people had a strict social plan called the _______________ system. There were _______________ castes of people. If one tried to rise above his caste, he became and outcaste, or an _______________.

Multisyllabic words Spelling Test

Score: ____________________

Date: ____________

		A	B	C	D
1.	________	elenmentary	elementary	ellementary	ellenmentary
2.	________	vehaclle	vehacle	vehicle	vehiclle
3.	________	miniatture	minaitture	minaiture	miniature
4.	________	prrubability	prubability	prrobability	probability
5.	________	oportonity	opportonity	opportunity	oportunity
6.	________	substitute	subsctitute	sobstitute	subsstitute
7.	________	varreity	variety	varriety	vareity
8.	________	litterature	literature	litteratore	literatore
9.	________	ellevator	elevatur	ellevatur	elevator
10.	________	Pennsylvanai	Pensylvania	Pennsylvania	Pensylvanai
11.	________	ravoilli	ravoili	ravioli	raviolli
12.	________	cafeteria	caffeterai	caffeteria	cafeterai
13.	________	mosiac	mossiac	mosaic	mossaic
14.	________	toxed	tuxd	tuxed	toxd
15.	________	metteurite	metteorite	meteorite	meteurite
16.	________	fasscinate	fascinate	fasssinate	fassinate
17.	________	cylander	cyllander	cylinder	cyllinder
18.	________	inttermedaite	inttermediate	intermedaite	intermediate
19.	________	centennail	centennial	centenial	centenail
20.	________	curoisity	curiosity	curroisity	curriosity

Score: ____________________

Business English: Common spelling mistakes

Date: ____________

First, circle the correctly spelled word or phrase. Then write a short definition on the line plus part of speech e.g. (n) for noun or (adj) for adjective.

		A	B	C	D
1.	______________	acummodate	acommodate	accommodate	accummodate
2.	______________	a lut	a lot	a llot	a llut
3.	______________	all raght	al raght	all right	al right
4.	______________	dephfinitely	dephinitely	deffinitely	definitely
5.	______________	maintenance	mainttenance	miantenance	mianttenance
6.	______________	miscpell	mispell	maspell	misspell
7.	______________	menmentto	memento	mementto	menmento
8.	______________	minussule	minuscule	minusscule	minusssule
9.	______________	nesesary	necesary	necescary	necessary
10.	______________	occurrance	occurrence	ocurrence	ocurrance
11.	______________	ocasoinally	ocasionally	occasoinally	occasionally
12.	______________	paxel	pixel	pixell	paxell
13.	______________	privileje	privilege	prrivilege	prrivileje
14.	______________	prronunciatoin	pronunciation	pronunciatoin	prronunciation
15.	______________	reseive	recieve	receive	resieve
16.	______________	restaurateur	restuarateur	resstuarateur	resstaurateur
17.	______________	schedolle	schedule	schedole	schedulle
18.	______________	separate	sepirrate	sepirate	separrate
19.	______________	tomorow	tomorrow	tumorow	tumorrow
20.	______________	troly	truly	trruly	trroly

9th Grade Spelling

Score: ____________

Date: ____________

		A	B	C	D
1.	______	comunication	communication	communicatoin	comunicatoin
2.	______	annooncer	anouncer	announcer	anooncer
3.	______	comnmentary	conmentary	comentary	commentary
4.	______	accent	acent	asent	acsent
5.	______	colleague	collaegue	colaegue	coleague
6.	______	apirent	aparent	appirent	apparent
7.	______	alude	allude	alode	allode
8.	______	agrescive	aggressive	aggrescive	agressive
9.	______	immerse	imerce	imerse	immerce
10.	______	illusoin	illusion	ilusoin	ilusion
11.	______	colaborate	culaborate	cullaborate	collaborate
12.	______	aplaince	apliance	appliance	applaince
13.	______	collisoin	colisoin	colision	collision
14.	______	acescory	accessory	acessory	accescory
15.	______	imacolate	imaculate	immaculate	immacolate
16.	______	accomulate	accumulate	acumulate	acomulate
17.	______	allegaince	alegaince	alegiance	allegiance
18.	______	aggravate	agravate	aggrivate	agrivate
19.	______	colapce	collapse	colapse	collapce
20.	______	illuminate	iluminate	ilominate	illominate

Sustainability - Global Warming - Climate Change

Score: ______________

Date: ____________

This is a spelling worksheet to check your spelling and then your understanding of key words to do with sustainability, climate change and global warming,

		A	B	C	D
1.	________	Ozone Layerr	Ozone Leyerr	Ozone Leyer	Ozone Layer
2.	________	Sustainability	Sustianability	Susstainability	Susstianability
3.	________	Deforestation	Defforestatoin	Deforestatoin	Defforestation
4.	________	Renewable Resoorces	Renewablle Resoorces	Renewablle Resoorces	Renewable Resources
5.	________	Non Renewablle Resources	Non Renewable Resoorces	Non Renewablle Resoorces	Non Renewable Resources
6.	________	Cllimate change	Climate chanje	Climate change	Cllimate chanje
7.	________	Habitat louss	Habitat los	Habitat lous	Habitat loss
8.	________	Trropical rian forest	Tropical rain forest	Trropical rain forest	Tropical rian forest
9.	________	Recycllang	Recyclang	Recycling	Recyclling
10.	________	Carbon doixide	Carbon dioxide	Carrbon dioxide	Carrbon doixide
11.	________	Metthine	Methine	Methane	Metthane
12.	________	Grenhoose gas	Greanhouse gas	Greenhouse gas	Grenhouse gas
13.	________	Hydrroflurocarbons	Hydroflurocarbons	Hydrophlurocarbons	Hydrrophlurocarbons
14.	________	Sulphur hexophluoride	Sullphur hexofluoride	Sulphur hexofluoride	Sullphur hexophluoride
15.	________	Nittroos oxide	Nitroos oxide	Nittrous oxide	Nitrous oxide
16.	________	Fossil Fuels	Fousil Fuels	Foussil Fuels	Fosil Fuels
17.	________	Transpurt	Transport	Trransport	Trranspurt
18.	________	Indostry	Inducstry	Indusstry	Industry
19.	________	Agriculture	Agricolture	Agrricolture	Agrriculture
20.	________	Pallm Oil	Pallm Oal	Palm Oil	Palm Oal

Score: ___________

9th Grade Spelling List

Date: ___________

	A	B	C	D
1.	unpredictible	unpredictable	unprredictable	unprredictible
2.	trransportatoin	trransportation	transportatoin	transportation
3.	terrarium	terarium	terariom	terrariom
4.	terrase	terace	terase	terrace
5.	soportive	sopportive	suportive	supportive
6.	subteranaen	subterranean	subteranean	subterranaen
7.	subgecttive	subjective	subjecttive	subgective
8.	repurter	reporrter	reporter	repurrter
9.	regect	rejectt	reject	regectt
10.	progectile	prrojectile	projectile	prrogectile
11.	predictoin	prediction	prredictoin	prrediction
12.	porrtage	porrtadge	portadge	portage
13.	objecttive	obgective	objective	obgecttive
14.	injection	injecttoin	injecttion	injectoin
15.	indictnment	indicttnment	indictment	indicttment
16.	dictator	dictatur	dicttator	dicttatur
17.	degected	dejectted	degectted	dejected
18.	contradiction	conttradiction	contradictoin	conttradictoin
19.	conttradict	cuntradict	cunttradict	contradict
20.	congectture	conjectture	conjecture	congecture

9th Grade Spelling Words

Score: ______________________

Date: ______________

Circle the correct word and then write it correctly on the line.

		A	B	C	D
1.	______________	combine	combei	combie	cumbine
2.	______________	conference	conferance	confference	confferance
3.	______________	comunity	community	commonity	comonity
4.	______________	conttact	cuntact	cunttact	contact
5.	______________	cumpete	cumpette	compette	compete
6.	______________	concenttrate	consenttrate	concentrate	consentrate
7.	______________	convert	converrt	cunverrt	cunvert
8.	______________	comment	coment	comnment	conment
9.	______________	cuntrast	contrast	cunttrast	conttrast
10.	______________	compoond	compood	compound	compoud
11.	______________	conduct	conductt	condoctt	condoct
12.	______________	converrsatoin	conversatoin	converrsation	conversation
13.	______________	commute	commotx	comote	comute
14.	______________	conssumer	consumer	consomer	conscumer
15.	______________	constitutoin	constitution	consstitutoin	consstitution
16.	______________	complinment	complliment	compliment	compllinment
17.	______________	conttinent	cunttinent	continent	cuntinent
18.	______________	comonicate	commonicate	comunicate	communicate
19.	______________	condittion	conditoin	condition	condittoin
20.	______________	compossition	composition	compositoin	compossitoin

9th Grade Spelling Words

Score: ____________

Date: ____________

Select the letter of the word that's spelled correctly!

	A	B	C	D
1.	imporrtant	impurrtant	important	impurtant
2.	experience	experrience	experreince	expereince
3.	ignurrant	ignurant	ignorant	ignorrant
4.	entrance	enttrance	enttrence	entrence
5.	difference	diference	diferance	differance
6.	instence	insstance	instance	insstence
7.	absance	absence	abssence	abssance
8.	appearance	appaerance	apaerance	apearance
9.	intelijent	intellijent	inteligent	intelligent
10.	evadene	evidance	evidene	evidence
11.	pollotant	polutant	polotant	pollutant
12.	cllaerance	cllearance	claerance	clearance
13.	confidance	conffidence	confidence	conffidance
14.	confferance	conferance	confference	conference
15.	inssurance	insurance	inssurence	insurence
16.	ambulance	ambullance	ambullence	ambulence
17.	hesatant	hesitant	hessitant	hescitant
18.	conscistent	consistent	cunsistent	conssistent
19.	excelance	excellance	excellence	excelence
20.	persistent	perrsistent	perrsastent	persastent

Score: ____________

9th Grade WordSearch Puzzle

Date: __________

X	I	S	U	B	D	I	V	I	S	I	O	N	S	I	H
B	Y	S	M	P	V	O	K	P	V	P	V	U	P	N	E
S	P	Y	H	T	R	A	C	E	M	P	W	C	E	D	R
X	B	B	W	R	G	N	I	T	A	L	Y	O	C	E	I
S	T	R	A	T	O	S	P	H	E	R	E	N	U	F	T
C	D	E	C	L	A	R	A	T	I	O	N	S	L	I	A
G	P	X	D	H	I	B	E	D	K	X	N	C	A	N	G
P	R	L	C	I	C	A	U	G	H	T	D	I	T	I	E
N	I	U	E	O	I	D	C	Z	D	E	P	E	I	T	K
O	K	Z	M	T	K	N	Y	X	K	Y	X	N	N	E	N
O	R	E	C	B	L	N	S	I	Z	H	L	C	G	O	E
D	P	A	H	U	L	F	J	L	I	A	D	E	Z	X	P
L	C	B	N	I	N	E	H	E	F	Y	M	I	K	F	S
E	A	D	J	A	C	E	N	T	L	R	R	X	P	M	B
A	Q	C	H	R	G	T	A	Z	G	O	G	D	Y	G	I
V	I	R	G	I	N	I	A	V	H	F	B	P	S	A	G

SPECULATING	CONSCIENCE	SUBDIVISION	ADJACENT	HERITAGE
INDEFINITE	HORIZON	TRACE	NOODLE	ITALY
GRUMBLE	STRATOSPHERE	VIRGINIA	CAUGHT	CACTI
DECLARATION				

Write sentences using words from above. Look up words when you are uncertain of their meanings.

____

Score: ____________

Words You Should Know Already

Date: ________

Please *unscramble* the words below.

YEAST	VELVET	COMMITTEE	EQUINE	TENNESSEE	AUGUST
PANEL	OCTOBER	SUBSTANTIAL	FREIGHT	SENSE	DIMENSIONAL
DEDICATION	COORDINATE	EDITING			

1. SESENEETN _ _ _ _ E _ _ E _
2. HGETRFI _ _ _ _ G H _
3. DGNITIE _ _ I T _ _ _
4. EIMOTETCM _ _ _ _ I _ _ E _
5. GTAUSU _ U _ _ S _
6. SSNEE _ _ _ _ E
7. ERBOCOT _ _ _ O _ E _
8. ILMSNIDAONE _ I _ _ N _ _ _ _ _ _ L
9. TEAYS Y _ _ _ _
10. EVTEVL _ _ L V _ _
11. DTAIICDNEO _ _ D I _ _ _ _ _ N
12. RTNEODICAO _ _ _ R _ _ _ A T _
13. NAPEL _ _ _ E _
14. UEEIQN E _ _ _ _ E
15. ALSASUBITNT S _ B _ _ _ N _ _ _ _

Write sentences using words from above. Look up words when you are uncertain of their meanings.

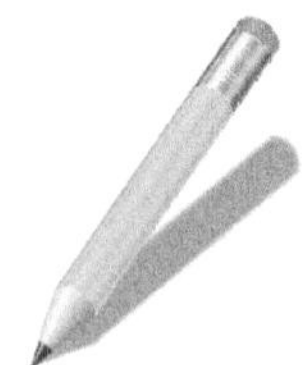

Score: ____________________

Words You Should Know Already

Date: ____________

Please *unscramble* the words below.

ENVIRONMENT	BRUISE	INFLUENTIAL	DUPLICATE	HIPPOPOTAMI	MERCURY
SUBHEADING	PERISHABLE	CONSTANT	AMBIGUITY	CERTIFICATE	FORGETTING
INFORMATION	ASTROLOGY	MISSISSIPPI			

1. TNACTOSN _ _ _ _ T A _ _
2. PMOPIOTIPHA _ _ _ _ _ _ O T A _ _
3. TAEFTIIRCEC _ _ _ _ I _ I _ _ _ E
4. AEICTLUDP D _ _ L _ _ _ _ _
5. SIMSSPSIIIP _ _ _ S _ _ _ _ _ P I
6. UISBER _ _ _ _ S E
7. RMRCEUY _ _ R _ U _ _
8. IUIFAETNLLN _ _ _ _ _ _ N _ I A _
9. TGOGENRITF _ _ _ _ E T _ _ N _
10. NORIVNTNEME E _ _ _ _ _ N _ _ N _
11. IFNROINTOAM _ _ F _ _ _ _ T I _ _
12. BASDGEHIUN _ _ _ H E _ _ I _ _
13. OTYRASGOL _ S _ _ O _ _ _ _
14. YIUTAMGBI _ _ _ _ U _ T _
15. IEPAEBRHSL _ E _ _ _ _ A _ _ E

Write sentences using words from above. Look up words when you are uncertain of their meanings.

____

____

____

____

____

Score: ____________________

Words You Should Know Already

Date: ____________

Please *unscramble* the words below.

MELON	MISSOURI	ARRIVE	ZOOLOGY	QUARREL	SUGGESTED
SOLEMN	TRILOGY	UPSETTING	PLUGGED	AUDIT	TERRIER
UNIVERSE	COMPLAINT	TANGERINE	EXCELLENT	NEEDLE	

1. GEUDGLP _ _ U _ _ _ D
2. GOIYTRL _ _ I _ _ G _
3. RIAREV _ _ R _ V _
4. NEANTIEGR _ _ N _ _ _ I _ _
5. TAOLICPMN _ _ M _ _ _ _ _ T
6. NLDEEE _ E E _ _ _
7. AUTDI _ U _ _ _
8. OYOOGLZ _ O O _ _ _ _
9. TIEERRR T E _ _ _ _ _
10. SUMOISIR _ _ _ _ _ U R _
11. UERRQAL _ U _ R _ _ _
12. TCXEELENL _ _ _ _ L _ E _ _
13. ETSEUSGDG _ U _ _ E _ _ _ _
14. LNMEO M _ _ _ _
15. MSELNO _ _ _ E _ N
16. INVERESU _ N _ V _ _ _ _
17. TTUINSEPG _ _ S _ _ _ I _ _

Write sentences using words from above. Look up words when you are uncertain of their meanings.

....

....

....

....

Score: ____________

Words You Should Know Already

Date: ________

Please *unscramble* the words below.

TERRIFIED	CONTROLLED	ARCHERY	MASSACHUSETTS	SERVANT	MEDIA
METEOROLOGY	ATTRIBUTE	AERODYNAMIC	SUFFRAGE	GENUINE	APPARENTLY
TROUT	VARIOUS				

1. AMIDE _ _ D _ _
2. NNEGEIU _ _ N _ I _ _
3. NRAEPPALYT A _ _ _ _ E _ _ L _
4. EAUTIBTTR _ T _ _ _ _ _ T _
5. SAETSSACTSM HU M _ _ _ A _ _ _ _ _ T _ S
6. HRERYCA _ _ C _ _ _ Y
7. TRVSNAE _ _ R _ _ N _
8. RERTDIIEF T _ _ _ I _ _ _ _
9. VIOUSRA V _ R _ _ _ _
10. AEIMCRNYODA A _ _ _ _ Y _ A _ _ _
11. ROTECLOLDN _ _ _ T _ _ L _ _ D
12. RUTTO _ _ _ _ T
13. FFESGU AR _ U _ _ _ _ G _
14. OGEELRYOM OT _ _ T _ _ R O _ _ _ _

Write sentences using words from above. Look up words when you are uncertain of their meanings.

Score: ______________________

Words You Should Know Already

Date: ______________

Please *unscramble* the words below.

PREVENTION	INSPECTION	MAGNETIC	SIXTY	REVISE	PREACHER
SIGNATURE	LANGUAGE	LITERATURE	PUPIL	PIONEER	PROVERB
SCIENTIST	POISON	PERMANENT	PERISH	REACTION	MATHEMATICS
KEPT	MINIATURE				

1. PTKE _ E _ _
2. PPLIU P _ _ _ _
3. SXIYT _ I _ _ _
4. TRPNOVINEE _ _ _ V E N _ _ _ _
5. RNAPETMNE _ _ _ _ _ _ _ E N _
6. SMTEMTCIAAH M _ T H _ _ _ _ _ _ _
7. SOOPNI _ _ _ _ O N
8. MINTCEGA _ _ G N _ _ _ _
9. RVEOPRB P _ O _ _ _ _
10. INOTAREC _ E A _ _ _ _ _
11. EROPINE _ I _ _ E _ _
12. SEIHRP P E _ _ _ _
13. TETRAILURE L I _ _ _ A _ _ _ _
14. OETISNCIPN _ _ S _ E _ T _ _ _
15. ULEAGGNA L _ _ _ _ _ _ E
16. HECPERRA P _ _ _ _ _ E _
17. UNRMAIETI _ _ _ I _ _ _ R _
18. ESSTCNTII _ _ _ _ N _ _ _ T
19. IEVERS R _ _ I _ _
20. ATNSGEIRU _ I _ _ _ _ _ R _

Write sentences using words from above. Look up words when you are uncertain of their meanings.

....

....

____

Words You Should Know Already

Score: ____________________

Date: ____________

Please *unscramble* the words below.

RICHER	INFECTION	LEGISLATIVE	PERCENT	PLENTY	PROFESSION
MONITOR	PARSLEY	SHORTEN	REPRESENT	NEUTRAL	REMEMBER
RECYCLE	RESIST	SLIDE	POLLUTION	PASSAGE	RELAX
MITTEN	PERPENDICULAR				

1. EENPRCT P _ _ _ E _ _
2. EIROONFSSP _ R _ _ _ _ _ I O _
3. UPINEEADLRRPC P _ _ _ _ _ _ _ _ _ A R
4. NRSPETEER _ _ _ _ E _ _ N _
5. SEGPAAS _ _ _ S _ G _
6. CREHIR _ I _ _ E _
7. REMEBMRE _ _ M _ M _ _ _
8. RUNELAT _ E _ _ _ _ L
9. RNSHOET _ _ O _ T _ _
10. EALXR R _ _ _ _
11. METTNI _ I T _ _ _
12. RTSISE _ _ _ I _ T
13. ALSRYEP _ _ _ S _ E _
14. EILILEVGATS _ _ _ _ _ _ L _ _ I _ E
15. NITPOULLO _ _ L _ _ _ _ O _
16. NONEICITF _ _ _ E _ _ _ O _

17. LIDES _ _ _ _ E

18. ELECCYR _ E C _ _ _ _

19. ETNLPY P _ _ N _ _

20. MOINROT _ _ _ _ T _ R

Write sentences using words from above. Look up words when you are uncertain of their meanings.

9th Grade Academic Vocabulary Test

Score:____________

Date:____________

no letters go in the gray boxes; 6 of the terms include two words

11 2 5 7 10 6 9 3 4 8

Across

3. a particular tendency or inclination; prejudice
4. the processes in which carbon moves and is stored in the ecosystem
5. a system of banks, chartered by Congress, to provide security for the economy
8. a mathematical phrase involving at least one variable and sometimes numbers and operation systems
9. the first speech given by a newly elected president
10. an antislavery campaigner in the 18th and 19th centuries
11. an equality involving an algebraic expression

Down

2. a part that goes before; a word or group of words to which a pronoun refers
6. a court ruling marking an important event or turning point in history
7. the murder of a prominent person
10. a figure of speech, reference or representation to a well-known person, place, event, literary work, or work of art

ASSASSINATION BIAS LANDMARK CASE ALGEBRAIC EQUATION BANKING SYSTEM CARBON CYCLE ANTECEDENT ABOLITIONIST INAUGURAL ADDRESS ALGEBRAIC EXPRESSION ALLUSION

9th Grade Spelling Practice

Score: ________

Date: ________

Circle the word that is spelled correctly and then write it on the line.

		A	B	C	D
1.	________	vindicattoin	vindication	vindicatoin	vindicattion
2.	________	indoctrinatoin	indocttrination	indocttrinatoin	indoctrination
3.	________	pollinatoin	pollination	polination	polinatoin
4.	________	mediattion	mediatoin	mediattoin	mediation
5.	________	fabricatoin	fabrrication	fabrication	fabrricatoin
6.	________	innovation	inovation	innovatoin	inovatoin
7.	________	alliteration	aliteration	aliteratoin	alliteratoin
8.	________	aspiratoin	aspiration	asspiratoin	asspiration
9.	________	segregatoin	segregation	segrregatoin	segrregation
10.	________	vocation	vocattoin	vocattion	vocatoin
11.	________	libattion	libatoin	libation	libattoin
12.	________	generration	generation	generratoin	generatoin
13.	________	intimidatoin	inttimidatoin	inttimidation	intimidation
14.	________	inaugurratoin	inauguratoin	inauguration	inaugurration
15.	________	cullmination	culmination	culminatoin	cullminatoin

Score:________
Date:_________

Spelling/Definition Test

Test student on correct spelling of words or have them write the meaning (in short form) of words.

Your Answers
1
2
3
4
5
6
7
8
9
10
11
12
13
14
15
16
17
18
19
20

Correct Spelling or Meaning If Incorrect
1
2
3
4
5
6
7
8
9
10
11
12
13
14
15
16
17
18
19
20

Score:________

Date:_________

Spelling/Definition Test

Test student on correct spelling of words or have them write the meaning (in short form) of words.

Your Answers	Correct Spelling or Meaning If Incorrect
1 ________	1 ________
2 ________	2 ________
3 ________	3 ________
4 ________	4 ________
5 ________	5 ________
6 ________	6 ________
7 ________	7 ________
8 ________	8 ________
9 ________	9 ________
10 ________	10 ________
11 ________	11 ________
12 ________	12 ________
13 ________	13 ________
14 ________	14 ________
15 ________	15 ________
16 ________	16 ________
17 ________	17 ________
18 ________	18 ________
19 ________	19 ________
20	20

Score:________

Date:_________

Spelling/Definition Test

Test student on correct spelling of words or have them write the meaning (in short form) of words.

Your Answers	Correct Spelling or Meaning If Incorrect
1	1
2	2
3	3
4	4
5	5
6	6
7	7
8	8
9	9
10	10
11	11
12	12
13	13
14	14
15	15
16	16
17	17
18	18
19	19
20	20

Score:________

Date:_________

Spelling/Definition Test

Test student on correct spelling of words or have them write the meaning (in short form) of words.

Your Answers	Correct Spelling or Meaning If Incorrect
1 ______	1 ______
2 ______	2 ______
3 ______	3 ______
4 ______	4 ______
5 ______	5 ______
6 ______	6 ______
7 ______	7 ______
8 ______	8 ______
9 ______	9 ______
10 ______	10 ______
11 ______	11 ______
12 ______	12 ______
13 ______	13 ______
14 ______	14 ______
15 ______	15 ______
16 ______	16 ______
17 ______	17 ______
18 ______	18 ______
19 ______	19 ______
20	20

Score:________
Date:_________

Spelling/Definition Test

Test student on correct spelling of words or have them write the meaning (in short form) of words.

Your Answers
1
2
3
4
5
6
7
8
9
10
11
12
13
14
15
16
17
18
19
20

Correct Spelling or Meaning If Incorrect
1
2
3
4
5
6
7
8
9
10
11
12
13
14
15
16
17
18
19
20

Score:________

Date:_________

Spelling/Definition Test

Test student on correct spelling of words or have them write the meaning (in short form) of words.

Your Answers
1
2
3
4
5
6
7
8
9
10
11
12
13
14
15
16
17
18
19
20

Correct Spelling or Meaning If Incorrect
1
2
3
4
5
6
7
8
9
10
11
12
13
14
15
16
17
18
19
20

Score:________

Date:_________

Spelling/Definition Test

Test student on correct spelling of words or have them write the meaning (in short form) of words.

Your Answers	Correct Spelling or Meaning If Incorrect
1	1
2	2
3	3
4	4
5	5
6	6
7	7
8	8
9	9
10	10
11	11
12	12
13	13
14	14
15	15
16	16
17	17
18	18
19	19
20	20

Score:________

Date:_________

Spelling/Definition Test

Test student on correct spelling of words or have them write the meaning (in short form) of words.

Your Answers
1
2
3
4
5
6
7
8
9
10
11
12
13
14
15
16
17
18
19
20

Correct Spelling or Meaning If Incorrect
1
2
3
4
5
6
7
8
9
10
11
12
13
14
15
16
17
18
19
20

GRADES TRACKER

Week	Monday	Tuesday	Wednesday	Thursday	Friday
1					
2					
3					
4					
5					
6					
7					
8					
9					
10					
11					
12					
13					
14					
15					
16					
17					
18					

Notes

GRADES TRACKER

Week	Monday	Tuesday	Wednesday	Thursday	Friday
1					
2					
3					
4					
5					
6					
7					
8					
9					
10					
11					
12					
13					
14					
15					
16					
17					
18					

Notes

Made in United States
Orlando, FL
27 March 2025

59898335R00070